MICHAEL HONE

CARAVAGGIO

His Life and Times

Cover: Caravaggio's *The Sacrifice of Isaac*

Revised and Enlarged Edition

© 2018

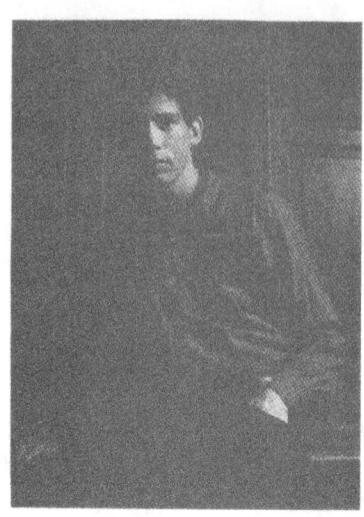

My books include: *Cellini, Cesare Borgia, Renaissance Murders, TROY, Greek Homosexuality, Roman Homosexuality, ARGO, Renaissance Homosexuality, Alcibiades the Schoolboy, RENT BOYS, Buckingham, Homoerotic Art (in full color), Sailors and Homosexuality, The Essence of Being Gay, Phallus, John (Jack) Nicholson, THE SACRED BAND, German Homosexuality, Gay Genius, SPARTA, Charles XII of Sweden, Mediterranean Homosexual Pleasure, CAPRI, Boarding School Homosexuality, American Homosexual Giants, HUSTLERS, The Bloomsbury Set* and *Christ has his John, I have my George: The History of British Homosexuality.* I live in the South of France.

DEDICATION

This book is dedicated to Cosimo de' Medici and his grandson Lorenzo *Il Magnifico*, fathers of Renaissance Italy.

CHAPTER ONE
Page 4

CARAVAGGIO: AN INTRODUCTION
Cellini, *The Musicians, The Martyrdom of Saint Ursula*, Cecco

The Boy Bitten by a Lizard

CHAPTER ONE

CARAVAGGIO: AN INTRODUCTION

Caravaggio was noted for his use of chiaroscuro to such a point as to be thought, by some, to be its inventor. Chiaroscuro is the contrast, often very strong, between light and dark, enforcing the three-dimensionality of objects. Around 90% of Caravaggio's life resided in the *oscuro*, the bleakness of which made his biography far more difficult than my last work had been, *Cellini, His Life and Times*. Despite the dark side of Cellini, the fact that he had murdered several men (stalking and knifing them from behind) and the even more disconcerting fact that he was a confirmed sadist towards women (confirmed by his own autobiography!), the *chiaro* portions of Cellini's life were by far the more important. Like Caravaggio, Cellini was an artist of genius, but one--and this was the winning point, for me, concerning Cellini--who worshipped the boys he loved. Throughout Cellini's autobiography we find these panegyrics that leave no doubt as to the erotic nights and equally languorous days spent with his young--at times incredibly young--lovers: "We are never apart, day or night," "We loved each other more than if we had been brothers," "My passionate love for the boy," "The prettiest face of anyone I have ever met in my whole life," "He's amazingly beautiful, and the great love he's shown me made me love him in return--almost more than I could bear," "His beautiful smile would have driven the gods themselves mad," "Extreme personal beauty" and "The most handsome young fellow in Rome."

What was engaging concerning Caravaggio was the *chiaro* of his first paintings, the eroticism found in the close-ups of certain works--here I'm thinking of his *The Musicians*--which show the boys' faces in the very throes of immanent orgasm, the eyes glazed over, the lips sensually parted, the tongue just visible and lascivious. Or the boys' shirts, in this and in other paintings--always boys, as his first painting of a woman came only in 1597 with his *Repentant Magdalene*--shirts at times undone to the waste, open on skin glistening through effort, perhaps sexual, the nipples erect, the underarms reeking of pheromones, the odor of sex so invasive that one can guess at the traces of sperm smeared somewhere over the lower belly.

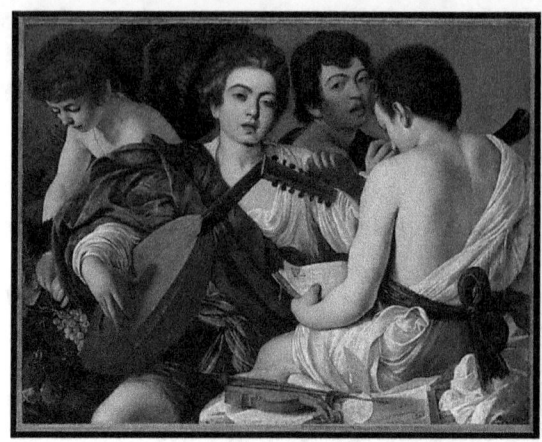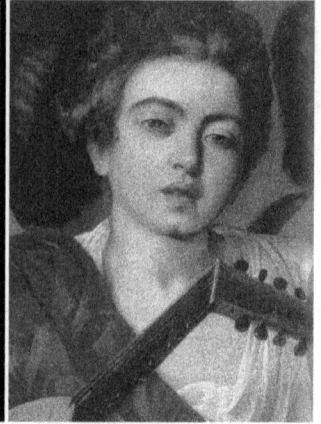

The Musicians.

But I was enthralled too by the *obscuro*, the blood gushing from the jugular of the virile male in his *Judith Beheading Holofernes,* as the knife is halted forever in mid-distance, as it cuts through the throat. Or the nearly naked soldier in *The Martyrdom of Saint Matthew,* sent to murder the saint so that the king of Ethiopia could have access to Matthew's niece: the horror being that one so young and virile would dare destroy one so old and helpless. Then there's the *Sacrifice of Isaac* in which the withered mind of Abraham pushes him to slit the throat of his screaming son, his hand stayed at the last moment by an angel. And *David and the Head of Goliath*, David holding up Goliath's severed head, the self-portrait of Caravaggio himself, one eye clearly dead, the other harboring a lingering thread of life. *The Beheading of John the Baptist* is of disgusting reality: his executioner, muscular and shiny with sweat, the ultimate in homoeroticism, leans over the saint whose head he holds firmly against the floor, while blood spurts from the severed throat. (Caravaggio signed himself--Michelangelo--in the saint's blood, the only time he ever signed one of his works of art.) But the worst is *The Martyrdom of Saint Ursula*: A withered old man, unable to achieve his ends with a young woman, shoots her in the breast with an arrow at pointblank range. Ursula looks down at the wound, as if in wonder that she has been pierced and that blood is flowing. It makes me, too, wonder if the painting inspired the makers of the film *Munich* in which men come upon a female terrorist who, to escape death, offers herself naked. She's shot three times in the breast from close range and, like Ursula, looks down at the blood that begins to trickle from the wounds, as intrigued at the saint, and remains so until a final bullet is lodged in her brain.

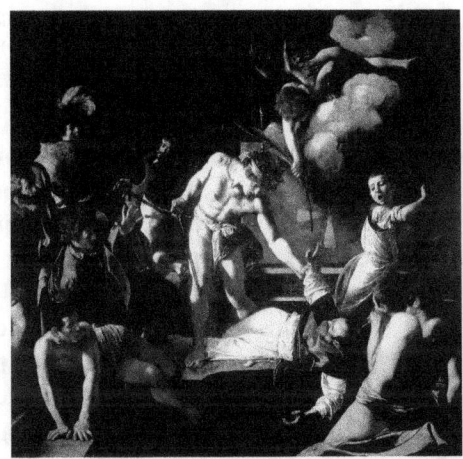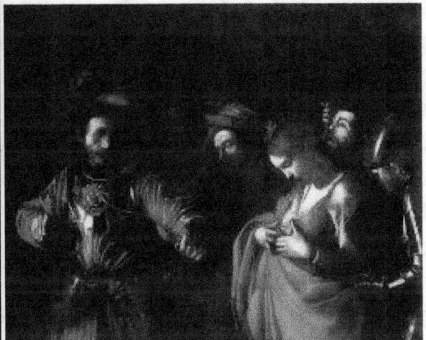

The Martyrdom of Saint Matthew and *Martyrdom of Saint Ursula* (the arrow extremely hard to see, alas).

My heart skips a beat and my breath gasps before the bloodletting in Caravaggio's works, taken to an extreme not even surpassed by today's snuff movies, artistry that Scorsese claims formed his own art.

Caravaggio worked alone, had no assistants, no workshop. He strode through the streets of Rome in the company of a wild bunch such as he, looking for action in the form of fights, his sword by his side and his dagger reassuringly in his belt. His eyes were wide-open and seeing, mean and blasé, his lips ridged. His motto was said to have been *nec spe nec metu*, without hope or fear. Someone compared him to a modern-day James Dean, but while Dean was a sissy who liked to take it up the ass, Caravaggio was a boy of his times, spoiling for a fight and learned in the arts of sword play. He was no sissy.

Historians writing about Caravaggio go off on tangents--interesting and instructive tangents--such as the supposed influence of this pope or that cardinal on the artist, none of whom had, in reality, the tiniest hold on Caravaggio, because if they had had such a role, how could one explain the painter's violence and the murders attributed to him? Popes, cardinals and priests were merely purveyors of the money that allowed the real heroes of those times--artists, writers and philosophers--to eat and drink to their fill, while accomplishing their works. The truth of Caravaggio is that once all we know about him is boiled down, reduced like a gallon of alcohol and a basketful of roses passed through a distiller, what we're left with is the wondrous scent emitting from a little residual dew, meaning that his life is basically unknown, but his paintings, the residual dew, are greater than those of any artist who has ever lived.

He lost nearly every male member of his family to the plague while still very young--his father at age 5, the rest at age 6--the plague that had killed over half of the population of Italy one or two generations earlier, around the 1350s, but reappeared from time to time to claim the survivors. This might have instilled a sentiment of abandonment, a child's first and greatest fear, a scar on the mind that pushes one incessantly from place to place, person to person, never at ease, never satisfied, always angry, violent, physically and sexually aggressive. Perhaps only a man of such unhinged and brutal appetites could create the works of this totally unique individual, stark, aggressive and sexually explosive segments of human life. This may partially explain the brutality of his nature, as well as the fact that the times in which he lived were in themselves ultraviolent, where even if a man looked at another for a nanosecond too long he might be challenged and put to death by sword. The origin of his violence even pushed one author to suggest that a catalyst for his brutal character stemmed simply from the chemicals used in his painting, lead white and vermillion, both of which are highly toxic.

Caravaggio was a man of great strength and a first-class swordsman. That he was also an artist whose delicate strokes created works of genius must not mask the fact of his indomitable virility, capable of downing a man with a blow--temporarily if done with the fist, life-threatening at the end of his sword. The proof of this was his slaying of the handsome Ranuccio Tomassoni in a duel. Caravaggio ran with a pack of toughs, armed to the hilt in a city where arms were forbidden. He and his goons drank and whored, pushed fellow revelers aside as they made their way through the alleys from tavern to tavern. They were constantly picked up by the Roman police, held the night and then freed as they had powerful friends, friends like Cardinal del Monte who was smitten by boys and who appreciated homoerotic art, bringing much of it into the Vatican (one of the reasons why the Vatican is, today, a must-see museum). Del Monte allowed Caravaggio to bed Cecco, a boy of only ten when he appeared as a prepubescent *St. John the Baptist*, a beautiful, brooding lad when painted a handful of years later in another *St. John.* Caravaggio and his ruffians broke windows, sang bawdy songs, hurled animal bladders filled with blood or ink at buildings, smeared excrement on door handles and, naturally, drew erect, usually discharging phalluses on walls. An unknown source had this to say at the time: "After a fortnight's painting he swaggers about for a month or two with a sword and like-minded friends at this side--Prospero Orsi, Orazio Gentileschi, Mario Minniti and Onorio Longhi--ever ready to engage in a fight or an argument, so that it is awkward to get along with him." To say the least. Another of his acquaintances, Agostino Tassi, was accused by a father of "repeatedly deflowering" his daughter! (Perhaps, like Aphrodite, her virginity continually rejuvenated by bathing off the shores of Cyprian Paphos.) For every outrage that I'll recount in this book, there may have been a hundred others unknown to us or too little known to relate or were covered up by the people looking out for him, the most important of which was Cardinal del Monte. We known that Caravaggio lived for his art, but it can be said that he lived too to impose himself, violently, on others. But unlike Cellini (6), he is not known to have beaten women or kicked small boys in the balls for fun.

He whored, but his preference was men, a choice far from unknown in the Florence of his epoch where men chose freedom over marital bondage, where one could take one's pleasure when and where one desired, with a boy or a man, free of nagging and the expense of a meal. This is what Andrew Graham-Dixon says in his wonderful *Caravaggio*: ''Caravaggio was capable of being aroused by the physical presence of other men. He could not have painted such figures in the way that he did if that were not so. Caravaggio's painting suggests an ambiguous sexual personality. On the evidence of his paintings he was neither heterosexual nor homosexual, terms that are in any case anachronistic when applied to his world. He was omnisexual.'' Most authors, other than Graham-Dixon, go out of their way to presume a man innocent of homoerotic yearnings and--even more--of committing homosexual acts, unless provided with the proof of their guilt by someone having spent the night under the perpetrator's bed, and even then they attribute his having sex with another man as ''a passing bisexuality'', ''youthful experimentation'', a momentary ''confusion of sentiments'', rapidly grown out of.

Boys at that time loved to dress to kill. Churches abounded in Renaissance Italy, and especially in Florence and Milan, perfect stages for a young sire to show off his splendid forms, silk-adorned chest, form-fitting trousers, elegance out to swoon the fair sex, a dagger at the belt and a sword ever handy, a youth's tools. For the daily, reliable and rapid purging of one's lust, there were bordellos, taverns with frisky and economically cheap servers, as well as back alleys where, indeed, all cats were grey in the absence of light, and a lad had but to pull the strings attached to the cloth that covered his private parts to take his pleasure with whomever engorged his manhood, or when he simply wished to relieve himself against a wall.

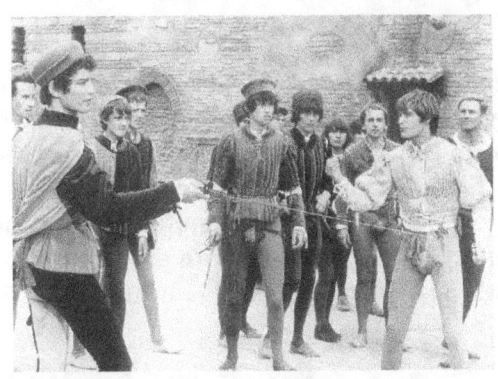

A lad had but to pull the strings attached to the cloth that covered his private parts to take his pleasure with whomever engorged his manhood or to simply piss.

Interlude

Love Conquers All

As in the joyful *Love Conquers All* we find Cecco again, a little older, here in the role of a very young *John the Baptist*, smiling, smirking, grinning, a pure boy (pure in the sense of authentic), with a boy's malice; puberty is nigh, and with it the answers to secrets and the discovery of physical joys. Totally erotic, the lad hasn't as yet taken to covering himself because he's still unaware of adult shame. The ram, like the satyr, is a symbol of lust and we, the viewer, can only rejoice in the newness of a lad's discoveries and new knowledge, and remember our own.

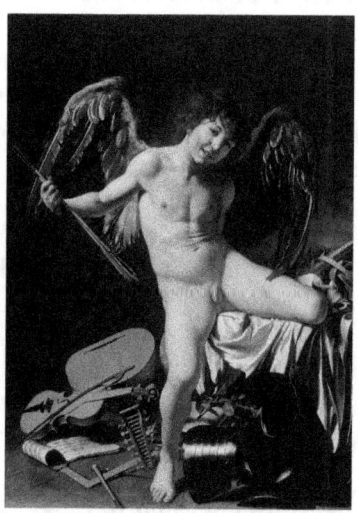

Love Conquers All

Sexual symbolism is seen everywhere in Caravaggio's works, from the lizard in *The Boy Bitten by a Lizard* to the sword in *David with the Head of Goliath*, both said, by some biographers, to represent the penis. It is nonetheless true that the boy in *Love Conquers All* does take the pose of Leda, her legs open, awaiting Zeus in the form of a goose, the long neck of which will eventually impregnate her with Clytemnestra and Helen (4). The details of the ram's horns and St. John's ear are stupefying.

10

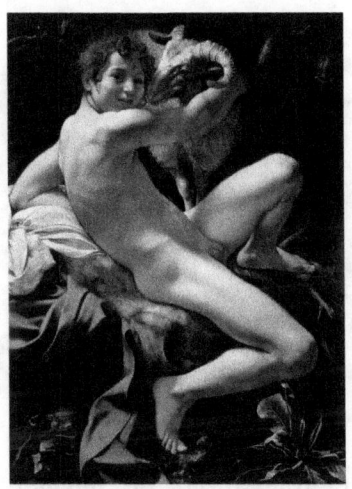

Cecco as *John the Baptist*

CHAPTER TWO

THE WORLD INTO WHICH CARAVAGGIO WAS BORN

Like a jewel, the life of Caravaggio must be placed in a proper setting, in this case the Renaissance. The lengthy excursion to follow will inform the reader of the men and the events that preceded the birth of Caravaggio, men as diverse as Cosimo de' Medici and da Vinci, thanks to whom we exist intellectually.

Man is stirred physically, mentally and, of course, sexually. Whether we like it or not, sex is the motor that rules the world, now as then. Cesare Borgia wanted armed power and sexual conquest, an easy equation for him as he possessed military genius and physical beauty; another condottiere whom we'll soon meet, Federico da Montefeltro, had lost an eye in battle and compensated by having his nose surgically hollowed out so he could see in all directions with but one eye. His might and wealth assured him a warming presence for his bed.

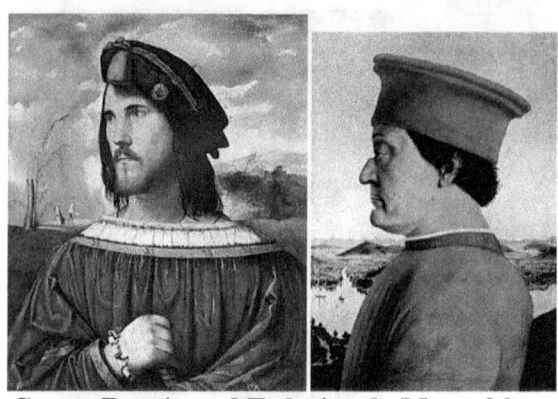

Cesare Borgia and Federico da Montefeltro

Sexual satisfaction was by far the norm in the man's world of the Renaissance, but not exclusively. Caterina Sforza, of Imola and Forlì, used her position as regent to put her stable boy into her bed, an extraordinarily handsome lad murdered by her subjects who found him wanting in class, only to be replaced by another even more handsome suitor, Giovanni de' Medici. But as might made right then as today, Caterina was conquered by Cesare Borgia who wanted her lands. He raped her before turning her over to his tavern companions. Cesare's sister Lucrezia Borgia was another free spirit who would know more love and the loss of love, debauchery and suffering, than mere mortals would know in several lifetimes.

Throughout this book I'll approach Renaissance sexuality more completely, but for now I'll limit myself to the intellectual and militaristic impulses of the times, and what better place to begin than with one of the bright lights of the period, the Florentine Cosimo de' Medici, grandfather of the future Lorenzo *Il Magnifico,* the star of the Renaissance.

The story of Cosimo begins to the north of Florence, in the city-state of Milan, ruled by Duke Philippo Maria Visconti, a hugely ugly and hugely fat recluse who kept to his fortress, out of the sight of those--ambassadors, kings, emperors and the like--who might judge his physical hideousness. He had a dream, that of becoming lord over as much of the land surrounding Milan as militarily possible, a dream that led him to attack the Romagne, home of tiny fiefdoms such as Forlì, Imola and Faenza. He also attacked the Florence of Cosimo de' Medici. He was paranoiac to the extreme, switching bedrooms as many as three times a night to avoid assassination. He murdered his older brother Gian Maria, a ruler of incredible cruelty who dressed his dogs to devour whomever he sicced them on. When Philippo Maria Visconti found his wife lacking in enthusiasm to be covered by his walruse-like blubber, he accused her of having an affair with a young page and had them both beheaded. He then married a girl whom he expulsed from the palace when, on the wedding night, the superstitious duke heard a dog barking--an evil omen. Before taking any decision he had his astrologers indicate the place and time for each of his actions. He fathered an illegitimate daughter, Bianca.

The attack of Duke Philippo on Florence pushed Cosimo to hire a mercenary, the extraordinary Francesco Sforza. Cosimo wanted Francesco to destroy the power of Milan but Francesco Sforza hesitated before entering the city-state because he had plans to marry Bianca and take over Milan without having to wage war. His plan worked, he married the beauty, but as Duke Philippo had not formally named him as his successor, Milan declared itself a republic on Duke Philippo's death, a mere hiccup for Sforza who garrisoned the town and had himself declared duke. But Sforza's contacts with Cosimo had been so humane and intellectually stimulating that Milan and Florence became friends. Cosimo backed Sforza financially to such an extent that Cosimo's palace became, literally, the Bank of Milan.

Venice, ever afraid of the hegemony of Milan, decided to send troops against both Florence and Milan. Florence appealed to Charles VII of France, a super power that made Venice withdraw simply by threatening to intervene. To thank Charles, Florence acknowledged France's age-old claim to Naples. Furious, Naples decided to go to war with Florence and sent troops to capture the city. Venice too decided to intervene again. Cosimo became literally sick due to the new circumstances and took to his bed. Then two miracles occurred. Naples had to withdraw its troops from the outskirts of Florence when France sent troops to make good its claim on Naples, and Venice had to withdraw its troops when Constantinople fell to the Turks, the greatest threat ever to Venetian trade. For added safety, Venice united with Florence and Milan and an era of peace descended over the former belligerents. To make doubly certain that peace would last, Cosimo sent the most precious of his possessions, a manuscript by Livy, to Ferrante, King of Naples--itself now safe thanks to the timely death of Charles VII. Ferrante was a humanist who loved ancient learning, as did Cosimo himself. Overjoyed, Ferrante promised eternal peace between Naples and Florence.

So here we have the powers that will concern this story as it unfolds: Milan, Florence, France and Naples--we can't count Venice because the Serenissima was too busy making money to really care what was going on outside its waters. Papal authority will remain inefficacious until the advent of Alexander VI, followed by Jules II. Then all hell will break out.

I began by referring to war and carnage. But Italy was far from the only country where we find the inhumanity of men. At the exact same moment, to the East, another despot reigned. Vlad the Impaler was known by his father's name, Dracul, meaning son of the dragon. His father ruled

Wallachia. He was a warrior who dedicated himself to the protection of Christians against the hordes of Ottomans of whom he is credited with impaling tens of thousands. As a boy he spoke Romanian and learned Greek, German and Latin, combat skills as well as geography, mathematics and science. Vlad and a younger brother, Radu the Handsome, were sent by their father to the Ottomans as hostages and there Radu converted to Islam. The Ottomans taught the boys warfare and horsemanship. Vlad's father was overthrown and Vlad's older brother, who should have succeeded his father, was blinded and buried alive. When Vlad eventually came to power in Wallachia he strove to increase both the defenses of the country and his own political power. He had the nobles he held responsible for his father and brother's murders impaled. When Turks arrived to reclaim tribute from Wallachia he requested that they remove their turbans in respect for his person. When they refused, he had the turbans nailed to their heads, killing them all. The Turks sent an army that Vlad defeated; the soldiers were impaled with the highest stake reserved for their general. The pope and the Venetians--whose trade had been disrupted by the Turks--were wild with joy at the news. But Vlad's little brother who had converted to Islam, Radu the Handsome, came at the head of Janissary battalions to destroy his Christian brother. In addition, he promised that the nobles in Wallachia who had lost their positions because of Vlad would recuperate their entire wealth. Vlad was thereafter assassinated under unclear conditions and beheaded. His reputation for evil spread through Germany and Russia. How much is true will never be known. He was said to have children roasted and then fed to their mothers, and to have the breasts of women cut off and forcibly fed to their husbands, before impaling them all. It is also reported that the Ottoman army turned back from the Danube, in horror, when they came across thousands of rotting corpses, all impaled.

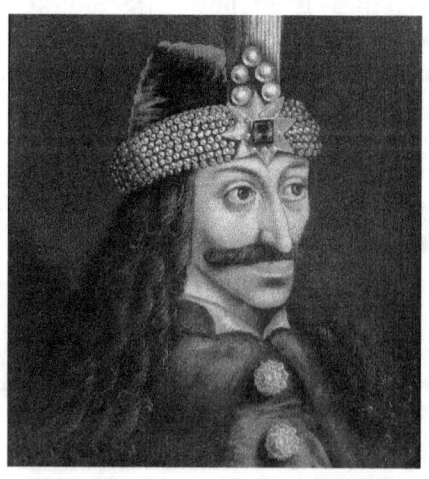

Vlad II Dracul, the Impaler.

After the fall of Rome the lights went out over Europe. New Christians like Charlemagne were proud of their ignorance, declaring that they were above grammar. Charlemagne gave a choice to conquered peoples, either they convert or they would fall to the sword. During just one morning 4,500 were beheaded when they hesitated. In Constantinople the first emperor to convert, Constantine, watched helpless while 3,000 Christians died under the sword of other Christians over the interpretation of the new faith, and during the Fourth Crusade the city itself was sacked and the inhabitants massacred when the crusaders failed to receive the monies the new emperor promised them. Saint Augustine, after a youth of depravity, declared that a child was already polluted in the womb, as he had been conceived through lust. People converted easily thanks to the promise of the afterlife, but went on with everyday violence in which thousands died in drinking brawls, sexual disputes and sports such as tournaments. Fear of disease and plague, invasion and famine, lightning and floods, dark forests of boars, bears and wolves, all combined to unite families in backward villages, where incest and a limited gene pool assured mental deficiency. Hunched over, afraid of every storm, medieval men lived out their existence is pure anonymity. There were no clocks, not even calendars among them, and even the century in which they lived was both unknown and of no importance. The Great Schism--a pope in Rome and one in Avignon--was unknown to the peasants who passed their days in perpetual toil, seeking out the church at the time of baptisms, marriages and deaths, alongside priests as ignorant as they. Illiterate, pockmarked, gullible, superstitious, for them there were no changes anywhere simply because they were unaware of all. They didn't even have surnames, because none were needed. Only later, when the ancient world was rediscovered, did the individual begin to emerge from the formless masses. Then they would take names in order to distinguish one from the other--the smithy became Smith, the tailor Taylor. Anonymity: nothing is known of the twenty-three generations it took to build the cathedral of Canterbury. But finally names emerged from the mist, those of da Vinci, Michelangelo, Botticelli, all thanks to the rediscovery of the ancient texts, a rediscovery and a rebirth: a Renaissance

The serpentine road from the Middle Ages through the Renaissance and on to Modern Times took centuries to unfold. It was this reemergence of the past, it was the heritage of a very distant Rome and Greece. It was the freedom of the human mind, a mind that turned to individual thought and rationalism over crass religious doctrine and its sandy foundation--faith. Humanism is thought to be anti-religion, but at the time the humanists were believers in religion who simply wanted to reform certain religious practices. Those who no longer believed in religions, and there were certainly few, were heretics and candidates for the stake--a real-life burning bush, a strong incentive not to wander too far from the beaten track. The belief in the separation of the church and state, and the right not to believe in certain dogmas at all, would come--albeit only partially--near the 1700s, with Voltaire.

Petrarch is not only the founder of humanism, but also the very inventor of the term Middle Ages. His endeavor was to free Middle-Ages man by bringing back such thinkers as the Roman Cicero (slaughtered at the hands of Marc Antony who wished to still Cicero's truths) (8). Along with the great Boccaccio (immensely readable to this very day), he also freed access to ancient works by reproducing them in the vernacular, Italian.

In Florence, Lorenzo *Il Magnifico*'s grandfather, Cosimo de' Medici, helped found humanism along with his friend Niccolò Niccoli. A banker, Cosimo offered Niccoli the funds necessary to send him far and wide, even to the Holy Land, in search of the ancient manuscripts that would bring the words of the likes of Plato into the very living rooms and libraries of the Medici, hundreds and hundreds of volumes. Each discovery that Cosimo made, each old text he unearthed, was like Howard Carter peering into the tomb of Tutankhamen. Cosimo employed forty-five copyists to spread the liberating concepts of the ancients, assisted by Niccoli who wore a Roman toga, to the embarrassment of his entourage. Greek studies became a part of Florentine university instruction and artists like Donatello and Brunelleschi built their art along classical lines. The distinction between Platonic truth and beauty and Plato's ideal republic diverged sharply with Cosimo's continued religious beliefs, among them that he was committing a mortal sin by applying, as a banker, usury to his loans. And then, each time civilization advances a step, it seemed (and seems) that something came (comes) along to set it back, forcing men on their knees before some god or other, because of man's lack of faith in himself: wars, disease, the horrors of the Black Death, civil strife, illness, sent (sends) men back in time to the first of the species, cave dwellers who feared fire and lightning.

The Renaissance was Florence, and Florence was the Renaissance. Why this should be so is unknown; perhaps the other great sites of the times, Naples and Milan, were too despotic, perhaps Venice too stable; Rome was out of the running because, until the intervention of Jules II, it was Hicksville, dirty, smelly and soiled by papal hangers-on and other such bovines. Traditionally, Florentine merchants vied with each other in their support of the arts. Ghiberti was commissioned to build the doors of the Baptistery of San Giovanni, a task that took twenty years. Brunelleschi somehow capped the Cathedral of Santa Maria del Fiore with a towering roof--the enigma being how the walls of the cathedral can bear the tons of weight--that is still the city's major landmark.

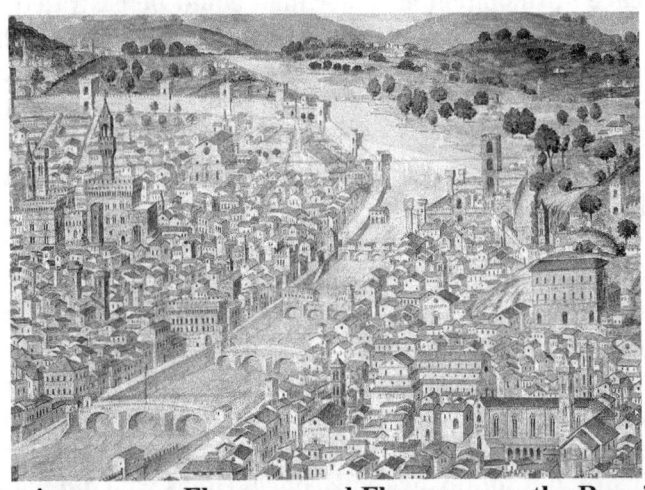

The Renaissance was Florence, and Florence was the Renaissance.

Today we make an industry of searching each other out; huge amounts of time and energy are dedicated to the enterprise. In Italy sex between males was but a strand of the social tissue. Men worked, studied and played together; they engaged in games and sports and cultural pursuits; they associated professionally or labored side by side. And when the mood and/or occasion was right, they shared a joint orgasm, a way of relief as was playing ball or swimming or horseracing, fencing or tournaments. It was natural in the way that sex should be. It was not the concentrated effort to rack up the greatest number of experiences or glee over the abundance of boys/girls one inseminated. The occasional release alongside the buddy who was at hand (literally) was the norm, in the same way that they ate and drank together.

It took the Dark Ages to make sodomy a crime. In ancient Rome male-male sex was simply an alternative means to pleasure. Amusingly, the exception to the prohibition of same-sex sex didn't apply to *boys* in Renaissance Italy, boys who could literally do anything they wanted with a male friend. It all fell under the category of "kids will be kids". For their parents, sex during adolescence was simply the discovery of one's body: what brought it pleasure, what brought it pain; what worked and what didn't; which zones were erogenous and which weren't. It was discovery--to the adolescent boy far more important than Columbus' fumbling onto the Americas. It was sexuality; it was in no way *homo*sexuality.

It was known that Cosimo's grandson, the great *Il Magnifico* himself, had a marked preference for boy buttocks. The preference was illegal but so prevalent that it was rarely prosecuted. But *rarely* prosecuted still meant that there were thousands of cases brought before the courts, which shows the prevalence of the phenomena. A man could be castrated for having sex with a boy (the ultimate cure!); boys 14 to 18 had to pay a fine of 100 lire; boys under 14 paid 50 lire. Foreigners could be legally beaten by whoever caught them *in flagrante delicto*, and if found guilty by a tribunal they could be burned at the stake. In reality no one was much bothered unless he raped a young boy or had sex with children. Consensual sex was more or less admitted; it was the coercive variety that was prosecuted.

Every boy wanted to marry a virgin. So boys who tried to seduce girls could find themselves in mortal danger as families were set on protecting their capital, their virgin girls, girls who served to form the alliances so necessary during the Renaissance. A girl deflowered was no longer an asset. To the contrary, she exposed her family to the open ridicule of the nobility. On the other hand it was accepted that boys needed physical release. The least harmful means of such release was between themselves, a measure that was silently but totally acknowledged. (Boys who did manage to seduce good girls were naturally congratulated by their pals and vaunted by their fathers.)

Naturally, boys could pay for sex in whorehouses or on the street, especially around the old market called the Mercato Vecchio. Alleys at night often saw girls lined up against walls while the boys humped them through the drop fronts of their skin-tight trousers, drop fronts attached by ribbons that could be rapidly undone.

As a banker Cosimo needed papal business due to the prestige that affiliation with the church represented to the world. He therefore cultivated certain men whom he felt might become pope (in the same way he had cultivated the condottiere Francesco Sforza who eventually became Duke of Milan and an enormously important ally). One such man was Parentucelli, a bookworm about whom it was said that anything he did not know was beyond human understanding. Cosimo lent him vast sums of money to buy manuscripts. When Parentucelli became Pope Nicholas V Cosimo helped him found the Vatican Library modeled after Cosimo's own. After Pope Nicholas came Pope Pius II, said to have been the Vatican's first humanist. He nonetheless loved wine, women and honors, all of which Cosimo provided him when he came to Florence. Pius tried to suppress a book he had written as a youth, *The Tale of Two Lovers*, supposedly full of erotic imagery, but through my twenty-first century eyes I see nothing sensual enough to offer the reader. The suppression of the book failed and it was a Renaissance best seller.

Another artist in Cosimo's service was Fra' Filippo Lippi. Headstrong and uncontrollable, his aunt placed him in a monastery when he was fifteen, where he later took his vows. When he discovered that he had a natural gift for drawing, he made his way to Padua to study art. A womanizer who fathered at least one known son, he was forced to flee to Ancona where, out sailing, he was captured by Moors and sold into slavery in Africa. Although human portraits were forbidden by Muslims, he drew the local caliph who was nonetheless so impressed that he freed him. Through the vagaries of life Lippi found himself in Florence working for Cosimo, but his taste for drink, women and bar fighting kept him from his art. In response, Cosimo had him locked in his studio where he ate and slept. He escaped and was found weeks later drunk and whoring. Cosimo tried a different tactic. He sent him into the country where, even so, Lippi met a nun he made pregnant. Cosimo arranged things through Pius II, the pope known for his erotic literature, who allowed the nun and the artist to marry. But before the marriage took place the nun's family poisoned him, although other sources believe he was poisoned by another mistress because of his interest in the nun. In any case, he *was* poisoned and Cosimo's grandson Lorenzo had a monument raised to him, built by Lippi's son who had, by then, become an artist just like his dad, Filippino Lippi.

Cosimo the great humanist died, but not before fathering Piero who in turn fathered the great Lorenzo *Il Magnifico*. The image of Cosimo that I love best is reported by an ambassador who, when he visited him, found him in bed between his two sons, Piero and Giovanni, one old man and two others middle-aged, all three suffering from gout.

Cosimo was succeeded by his son Piero called the Gouty, a disease that attacked the wealthy who could afford meat and rich sauces and who disdained vegetables considered peasant food or animal fodder. The result was the retention of uric acid which crystallized in the joints causing incredible pain. Piero married Lucrezia Tornabuoni, a chance for his son Lorenza because of her forceful nature and intelligence.

Piero was no banker compared to his father Cosimo. He rarely foreclosed debts and loaned funds to the likes of Edward IV of England who battled for years with Henry VI to see which of them would finally become king, running up horrendous bills and then, following victory, Edward died too young to repay them. Cosimo's squishy-squashy approach made enemies of every class from merchants to the nobility.

Piero attempted to shore up his relations with King Ferrante of Naples by sending Lorenza, superb from the heights of his seventeen years. Lorenzo did more than anticipated, charming the king out of his boots with his youthful candor, intelligence, sparkle and spunk.

Although a supposed humanist, Ferrante had a museum where he placed the dried cadavers of his enemies, pickled in herbs and dressed in what they wore when alive. When Ferrante suspected someone of plotting against him, he took him to visit his museum as a deterrent. Before their demise Ferrante locked his prisoners in cages and let them go insane before starving them to death.

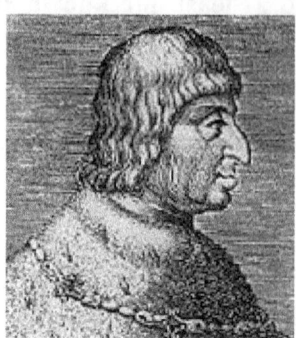

Ferrante (Ferdinand I) King of Naples

In Milan Francesco Sforza died and was replaced by his son Galeazzo Maria Sforza, age twenty-two. Galeazzo had been trained in combat by his father and was therefore feared. When the Duke of Ferrara decided, along with Venice, to take advantage of Piero's weakness as a leader by invading Florentine territory, Galeazzo sent 1,500 troops to Florence's aid. The Duke of Ferrara discovered that, although the citizens of Florence were unsatisfied with Piero, they would not rise up against him as the duke had been led to believe. So he retraced his steps and returned to Ferrara. The Doge of Venice continued on, however, forcing Piero to seek help from not only Naples and Milan, but also from a very feared condottiere, Federico da Montefeltro of Urbino, a city-state on the edge of the Romagna.

Federico da Montefeltro had been trained by Francesco Sforza. A condottiere sent by Venice, the equally feared (but aging) Colleoni, had also proved himself under the direction of Francesco Sforza. Colleoni had, in addition, married Francesco's daughter Battista. Along with Naples, Milan and Urbino, the Florentines themselves rounded up 3,000 soldiers that assembled in the main square of Florence, the Piazza della Signoria, under the direction of the very young Lorenza in full splendid armor. Galeazzo withdrew his forces for reasons he never explained and so it was that the troops of Federico da Montefeltro and the Venetian troops of Bartolommeo Colleoni met in battle, one that ended indecisively even though both sides claimed victory.

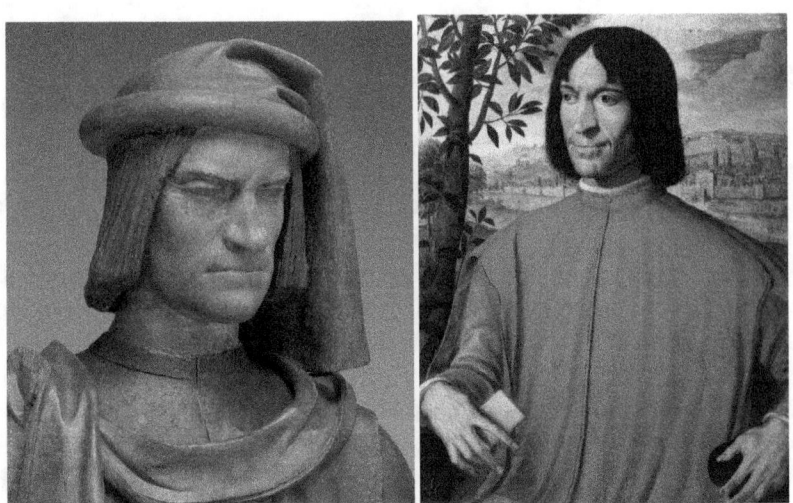
Lorenzo by Andrea del Verrocchio and by Girolamo Macchietti.

Much has been said about Lorenzo's ugliness, a nose so flattened it deformed his voice and destroyed his sense of smell. His hair was straight, his chin jutting, his eyes intelligent and piercing, dark and gentle. It is known that he attracted women who seem to have their own agenda in life's choices, masculine beauty being rarely one of them. Piero sent his wife Lucrezia to Rome to find a wife for their son. The choice fell on Clarice Orsini, beautiful but scoffed at by Lorenzo's friends behind his back as she was not known for her intelligence. The match was a step up for Lorenzo because the Orsini were nobles well entrenched in the church, many of whom had been cardinals and there had even been one Orsini pope.

Piero, too ill to do so himself, had Lorenzo organize a tournament in celebration of his betrothal, a contest between combatants on horses, armed with lances, aimed at unseating each other. It was said to have cost 8,000 florins while Clarice's dowry had been a modest 2,000 in comparison. There were banners and pennants and Lorenzo himself wore a cloak of white silk lined with scarlet. He rode a white charger given him by Ferrante King of Naples which made--given the back-stabbing tendencies of Italian politics--Galeazzo Maria Sforza green with envy. The wedding banquet lasted three days, with minstrels, tables laden with roast pig and 300 barrels of the best wine. Although Clarice and Lorenzo may never have been intellectually attuned, they were physically, as she gave him ten children. There is little doubt that more went on in Lorenzo's palaces and stables than girl-boy activities, and it is a fact that the laws against male-male encounters were relaxed to the point of near nonexistence while Lorenzo controlled Florence. The artists surrounding him--Donatello, da Vinci, Michelangelo--as well as teachers like the Greek and Latin scholar

Poliziano, were homosexuals, as were a number of Lorenzo's closest companions.

Italy throughout the ages, as much today as then, is known for its *jeunesse dorée.* Lorenzo had the best education possible, thanks to his grandfather Cosimo who allowed him to participate in the meetings of the Platonic Academy he had founded. His mother was versed in the arts and Lorenzo spent his life collecting the finest manuscripts, paintings, sculptures, coins and jewels--although, again, far less than Cosimo. He loved riding and hunting with falcons, giving full voice to dirty songs that amused his comrades as much as himself. He was not drawn to banking but he had the gift of appointing the right man to do the job in his place. He could be a brilliant conversationalist, an ardent churchgoer, and still slum the nights away in taverns and bordellos, ending the evening in the early hours by serenading the virgin sweetheart of one of his friends--after they had all fulfilled the lustful yearnings of their young flesh. He wrote poems, one of which warned of the ephemeral nature of youth, exhorting himself to make the most of what he had--and he had plenty. Again, then as today: the Italians have always been among the most sensual people on earth, and who could represent the beauty of the era better than the painter Botticelli whose *Primavera* is among the most gorgeous works of the human hand.

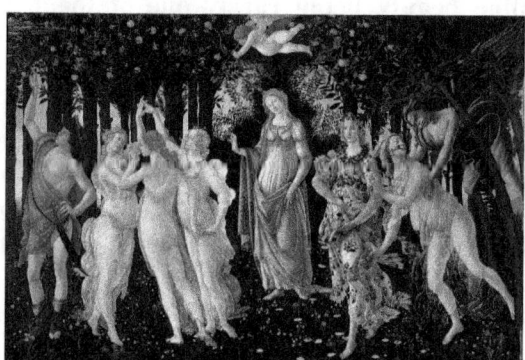

Primavera by Botticelli.

Lorenzo was a golden boy, yes, but one who was soon to know adversities that would have brought a lesser man to his knees.

A discussion of the church is necessary to the understanding of the geneses of Alexander VI. For a time the popes reigned in Avignon, a small pleasant town of beautiful fortifications and two beautiful rivers. They moved back to Rome in order not to lose the Papal States, land held from roughly 500 to 1870 when under Victor Emmanuel II Rome was captured as part of the final unification of Italy. At the time of Alexander VI the papacy held sway over a huge portion of Italy. The territory was expanded under two popes. The first pope was Alexander VI, whose reign saw the sudden rise of the ultimate warlord, his own son Cesare. The second was Julius II, during whose reign Cesare met his equally sudden end. The popes had only partial control over the Papal States, their influence varying according to the strength of the lord or count or prince who held this or that papal property.

Depending on the era and the pope, Rome was a dirty town with few inhabitants when compared to ancient times. Much of it was in ruins, the haunt of thieves and murderers, and pastureland covered even the ancient Forum of Caesar, Augustus and Cicero, now filled with goats and sheep. Bands of youths owned the streets, parading where they would, daggers and swords at the ready, beasts with ever-hungry bellies and ever-lustful loins. Cholera and dysentery left corpses where they expired, and the body parts of quartered victims, the remnants of executions, were hammered to doors or, in the case of heads, brandished on pikes. Smelly swamps and piles of refuse polluted the air, a far cry from sweet Avignon.

Pope Calixtus III was a Spaniard who had been in the service of King Alfonso V of Aragon (who also wore a second hat as Alfonso I of Naples). For vice-chancellor he chose his nephew, Rodrigo Borgia, a cardinal at age twenty-five, a Catalan like Calixtus, and the future Alexander VI.

At the death of Calixtus Rodrigo helped to elected the next pope, Pius II, after the usual conclave during which promises of wealth or important positions, such as vice-chancellor, were bantered about in the conclave latrines, the only private area for secret negotiations. In thanks, Pius kept Rodrigo on as vice-chancellor, the most substantive function after the pope, one in which a man could gain unheard-of wealth by accepting bribes that covered literally every aspect of human congress, especially sexual, from divorce to incest. Pius tried to limit what the historian Johann Burchard called Rodrigo's "endless virility." Burchard was responsible for the organization of ceremonies under Pope Pius, and thusly in an excellent possession to claim that Rodrigo organized frequent orgies, one of which, known as the Banquet of the Chestnuts: Johann Burchard, a major chronicler during the Italian Renaissance, was the Borgia Master of Ceremonies, responsible for the preparation of festivities. He wrote in his diary *Liber Notarum*, in Latin, that the orgy took place in Cesare's Palazzo Apostolico on the 30th of October 1501: "Fifty honest prostitutes, called courtesans, danced after dinner with the attendants and others who were present, at first in their garments, then naked. After dinner the candelabra with the burning candles were taken from the tables and placed on the floor, and chestnuts were strewn around, which the naked courtesans picked up, creeping on hands and knees between the chandeliers, while the Pope, Cesare, and his sister **Lucrezia** looked on. Finally, prizes were announced for those who could perform the act most often with the courtesans, such as tunics of silk, shoes and other things." William Manchester in his *A World Lit Only by Fire*, wrote: "Servants kept score of each man's orgasms, for the pope greatly admired virility and measured a man's machismo by his ejaculative capacity.... After everyone was exhausted, His Holiness distributed prizes...." (9)

The next pope was Eugenius IV, quickly followed by Sixtus IV who kept Rodrigo on as vice-chancellor, again thanks to his work in assuring the pope's election. Rodrigo extended his palace and enriched its furnishings and his clothes. Sixtus awarded him with bishoprics and abbeys, sources of more wealth still. During this period Rodrigo returned to Spain for an extended visit. On his way back his ship was wrecked off the coast of Tuscany and he was taken to Pisa to recover from his close call with death. There, at a banquet in his honor, he met Vannozza de' Catanei, the mother of his future children. In very quick succession she gave him Cesare, Juan, Lucrezia, Jofrè and Otaviano. In return, Rodrigo gave Vannozza a series of complaisant husbands and great wealth. These six were, however, only part of the brood he fathered with other acquaintances.

When Cesare was eight, Rodrigo moved all of his children to the home of his Spanish cousin Adriana da Mila, more qualified to raise them as she was of noble birth and would instruct them in the ways of the aristocracy. Adriana's son married a beautiful girl known as La Bella whom Rodrigo immediately took as his mistress.

The next pope, Innocent VIII, was known as the Rabbit for his lack of authority. Bands of youths, armed with daggers and swords, ruled the streets of Rome, stealing, raping and murdering to such an extent that the cardinals were forced to place guards with crossbows and artillery at their windows and on the roofs of their palaces. The new pope soon fell ill and died, but not before making Lorenzo *Il Magnifico*'s son Giovanni, age thirteen, a cardinal, a cardinal who would one day become Pope Leo X. The cardinals who came to the Vatican to replace Innocent VII met in conclave, now decided to elect a strong pope who would bring order to Rome.

Following the usual bargaining, during which wagonloads of gold, silver, jewels and precious furnishings and tissues were loaded at the Borgia palace and unloaded at the residences of nearly all of the cardinals (a few were said to have refused the bribes), Rodrigo Borgia became Pope Alexander VI. The truth of the bribes will never be known, and anyway, those who ran against him for pope were at least equally wealthy and equally inclined to bribe whomever they could.

Rodrigo *was* virile, producing many legitimatized children (as well as being the first pope to ever recognize his bastards) on his main mistress, Vannozza de' Catanei, of whom two were to become world famous, a daughter, Lucrezia, and a son, Cesare, an extremely evil warrior. He had at least four other children he did not recognize officially, but all his offspring and mistresses were abundantly cared for. Alexander was sensual, fun loving, certainly good to his children, a sugar-daddy papa, extremely tolerant, ruthless, courageous, and an administrator of genius.

He and his children spoke Spanish when together, but they all knew Italian, French and Latin. Cesare was destined for the orders, a destiny he hated as he hated his brother Juan who was marked for a military career, one Juan loved but was not good at--or at least not as good as Cesare would show himself to be. Juan was clearly Alexander's favorite, another supposed reason for Cesare's hatred. As virile as his father, slim waisted and certain of his sex appeal, Juan swaggered through the streets of Rome in what can only be described as gorgeous attire, a cloak of gold brocade, jewel-encrusted waistcoats and silk shirts, skin-tight trousers with drop fronts--cloth attached by ribbons that would free a man's loins when he wished to piss or fuck. This beautiful, gorgeously clad body, with 30 golden ducats still in his belt purse, was fished up from the Tiber, to the grief-stricken horror of his father who locked himself away from public view for three days. The death freed the way for Cesare to renounce his vows, having been made cardinal at age 18. Alexander never confronted his son with the murder of his favorite boy, but that he was guilty was silently acknowledged by nearly all. On the morning of the murder, just before sunrise, men were seen leading a horse with a body strapped over its back to the river edge, untie and then caste it into the middle. They were accompanied by another man on a white charger, his gold spurs reflecting the moon's glow. The men, said the witness, spoke in very low voices ... in Spanish. So it was Cesare ... unless ... unless, thought some, it was his other brother, Jofrè.

It's not clear at exactly what age Jofrè married but he was thought to be 12 and his wife Sancia 16. As puberty was far later in the Renaissance than today (around ages 15 or 16 then) he was unwilling to consummate the union--through a lack of libidinous testosterone. His brothers took over the task for him, however, an experience that was not necessarily grueling for the young girl as she was rumored to have had many lovers before arriving in Rome. At any rate, some historians place their bet on Jofrè as his brother's assassin, out of jealously, even though, in reality, Jofrè played only a minor role in the uncoiling events attached to the Borgias. At Alexander's death he was made Prince of Squillace, a vassal town of Naples where he lived until he died, having produced four children of his own.

Charles VIII entered Italy on his way to occupy Naples. His stopover in Rome was the first test of Alexander's exceptional intelligence. Alexander withdrew to Castel Sant'Angelo with all his possessions, including his bed. Romans fled to the countryside. Charles tried to calm the

Romans by telling them that his army wouldn't take an egg without paying for it. So numerous were Charles' men that they took six hours to file through the gate of Santa Maria del Popolo. They may not have stolen a single egg, but they stole everything else that hadn't been battened down, reportedly cutting off fingers when rings refused to budge. They raped any woman silly enough to have not already fled the city. They killed as well, especially the Jews. Alexander finally agreed to a meeting that took place in the papal palace. Charles is reported to have rushed to him and was prevented from a third genuflection by the pope who stopped him in mid-kneeling, giving him the kiss of peace on the lips. As Charles and his troops had brought syphilis into Italy, the kiss could not have been hygienic.

Syphilis may have been introduced into Europe by Christopher Columbus but this seems questionable as Columbus discovered the Americas in 1492 and the first cases of the disease were recorded in 1494 in Naples during Charles' invasion. How it could have spread so rapidly is one question, another question is why it wasn't present before Charles entered Naples, present in Paris for example. (At that time it was known, in French, as *le mal de Napoli*.) At any rate Charles had it and soon Cesare would be disfigured by its terrible scarification. Luckily for Charles, back in Paris he would knock his head against a doorframe and fall into a fatal coma, at age 28--thusly sparing him of the ravages of the disease. But for the moment he's kissing the pope. Charles, despite his extreme ugliness, had at least two different women a day, and in his baggage he carried a book of pornographic sketches and paintings of intercourse he had had with a few select beauties. Alexander successfully bypassed Charles' request that he recognize his claim to Naples, but the French king did insist on having Cesare as a traveling and hunting companion--a hostage to make certain that the pope kept his troops in their barracks. Alfonso II of Naples abdicated in favor of his son Ferrante II who fled Naples, leaving the city wide open for Charles. On the way there Cesare hung back on his horse and then took French leave, leaving the king beside himself with fury. (We'll revisit Charles in a moment in another context.)

Alexander had given Lucrezia Giovanni Sforza for husband, but discovering that the boy was a spy for Milan, Alexander decided to annul the marriage in favor of Alfonso of Aragon who was a member of the royal family of Naples and also Sancia's brother. After the slaying of Juan, Giovanni feared that Cesare would kill him too in order to further the ties between the Borgia and Naples. So he easily gave in, especially when he was told that he didn't have to reimburse Lucrezia's dowry of 31,000 ducats. He nonetheless spread the rumor that Alexander wanted the annulment so he could have Lucrezia for himself, and he bruited that he knew for a fact that Cesare had enjoyed his sister on many occasions. When Alexander informed him that he would have to sign a statement saying that he was impotent, he answered that he had had Lucrezia a thousand times. As additional proof of her innocence, Lucrezia was examined and found to be *vergo intacta*. In reality, she was six months pregnant and would give birth to a stillborn child say some sources, but most think the child lived and was named Giovanni, a boy Lucrezia raised, stating that he was her half-brother.

The boy responsible for her pregnancy was a handsome Spanish valet, Pedro Calderon, whom she lovingly called Perotto. In a frenzy of rage Cesare chased him through the palace until the lad sought shelter within the robes of Alexander VI himself. The pope tried to protect him but Cesare slashed at the boy through the robes, literally cutting him to pieces. The body was caste into the Tiber, along with the bodies of those aware of the scandal.

Alfonso and Lucrezia married and the wedding was consummated.

After the death of Cosimo his son Piero oversaw affairs in Florence, thusly establishing the reality of Medici control over the Florentine city-state. But as he was weak in mind and body, that control nearly ended with him. The city-state of Ferrara, to the north of the Romagna, sent troops to take over Florentine territory, as did the Doge of Venice under the generalship of the condottiere Bartolommeo Colleoni. Florence requested the help of the condottiere of Urbino Federico da Montefeltro. Once the Duke of Ferrara learned that the Florentines would not rise up against Piero as the duke had been assured, he withdrew to Ferrara. The battle between Venice and Urbino ended in a draw.

Galeazzo Maria Sforza, Duke of Milan, was thought to be a psychopath who didn't hesitate to tear off a man's limbs with his own hands or rape a woman, noble or not. His sexual appetite was hard to appease but once his lust fulfilled, the woman was handed to his entourage for their needs. He detested poachers, strangling one to death on a rabbit pushed down his throat and another was nailed inside his coffin and then buried alive. A priest who predicted Galeazzo would have a short life was starved to death. Galeazzo was finally brought down by three conspirators, one of whom was a very young man named Girolamo Olgiati who, thanks to Galeazzo's library to which the duke gave him access, was able to read the lives of Brutus and Cassius and how they tried to bring republicanism back to Rome through the assassination of Caesar (a perfect example of how the ancient texts formed the Renaissance mind). That was his ideal for Milan. A second conspirator, known only as Lampugnano, had obscure motives concerning land deals. The third conspirator was Carlo Visconti whose sister had been dishonored by the duke, a motive of importance today but at the time everyone was throwing his daughter or wife at Galeazzo in the hope of gaining profit. They met in church. Who struck first is in question, but the version I prefer has Visconti (the boy whose sister was raped) on his knees as if requesting a favor as the duke walked down the nave. When Galeazzo paused to listen to him, Visconti plunged his dagger into the duke's genitals. The other men followed suit. Galeazzo, at age 32, was dead before he hit the ground. The three assassins, certain of public support, did not bother to hide. Instead of thanking them, the citizens of Milan killed Lampugnano instantly and then dragged his body through the streets; the other two were caught later by Galeazzo's guard and their genitals were cut off and stuffed into their mouths before they were disemboweled, quartered and decapitated. As he was dying one of the three is reported to have shouted out, ''Death is perhaps terrible, but honor and glory are eternal!'' Which may be true as I'm retelling the story *500 years* after the event.

The condottiere Bartolommeo Colleoni, mentioned above, was a Renaissance exception to all of this violence. He was not known for treachery and he didn't rape, nor did he kill without reason. He tended to the vast lands the Venetians accorded him when not leading Venetian armies. He left his fortune to his army, and funds to finance an equestrian statue in his honor.

By far the most impressive condottiere of the period was Federico da Montefeltro. He was a Renaissance man, the possessor of a truly wonderful study done in *trompe-l'oeil*. He's thought to have killed his stepbrother Oddantonio, made easy by the people of Urbino who were unhappy with his reign. Federico took his place as count. He inspired loyalty among his men, sharing his gains as condottiere with them. Because his fees were high, he was able to enrich Urbino. He had surgeons remove part of his nose so that he could see in all directions with the eye remaining him, the other having been lost in a tournament, as mentioned. He fought for Florence, for Milan, for Naples and then against Florence before the Treaty of Lodi brought peace to the three city-states. The Treaty ended quarrels concerning the boundaries between the belligerents and confirmed the position of each duke, prince, count, doge or what have you, as the head of his particular city. It was not only signed by the three city-states, but also by Venice and the Papal States. The Treaty came to an end with the invasion of Charles VIII on France. After the death of Francesco Sforza, Montefeltro assisted Francesco's son Galeazzo Maria Sforza in governing Milan.

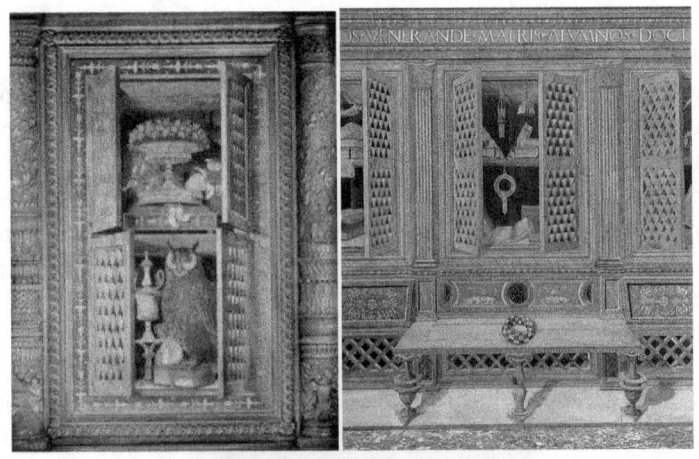

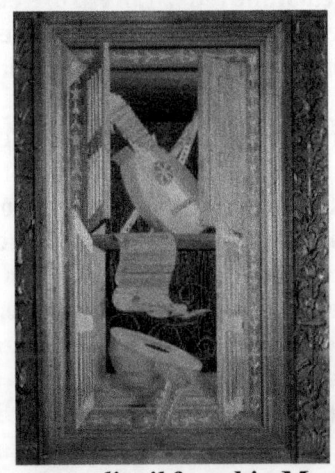

Examples of the *trompe-l'oeil* found in Montefeltro's studio.

At the death of Piero, Lorenzo was asked by the city nobility to take his place, which he did at age twenty, bowing modestly before the aged men standing before him. His first guest to his palace was Galeazzo Maria Sforza, accompanied by his soon-to-be-famous daughter, Caterina. Unknown to the nobles who requested his leadership, Lorenzo, fearing that he would be brushed aside as being too young and inexperienced, had sent messages to Galeazzo requesting troops, should he be forced to take power through arms. Galeazzo answered by putting a thousand men on the road to Florence. To thank him, Lorenzo put at Galeazzo's disposal every culinary, artistic and erotic pleasure at his disposal. Galeazzo returned to Milan decided to rebuild the city and stock it with art along the lines of Florence. Italy being Italy, Ferrante, King of Naples, became jealous of Lorenzo's influence over Galeazzo. This was Caterina's first visit to

Florence, the city in which she would turn to Christ when too old to receive lovers, the city in which she would die.

Lorenzo met with the new pope, Sixtus IV, and is said to have impressed the old man by his youthful vigor, although not enough so that Sixtus would give Lorenzo's brother Giuliano a cardinal's hat (Sixtus did, however, give six hats to his six nephews). Sixtus compensated by giving Lorenzo a splendid head of Augustus to the fury of Galeazzo he wanted it. Galeazzo was becoming less sane each day and, luckily for all, he was soon assassinated.

Young Lorenzo's first military sortie was against nearby Volterra that was under Florentine influence, the cause of which was a dispute over trade dues owed Florence. Lorenzo chose the famous Federico da Montefeltro to take the city, which he did, losing, alas, control over his soldiers who sacked, raped and killed hundreds. Lorenzo went to the town to offer his excuses and make amends by handing out money. Lorenzo knew it was a situation that his grandfather and father would have defused before an eventual massacre.

Sixtus IV, who had found Lorenzo to be a darling boy, asked him, as head of the Medici banking system, for a loan of 40,000 florins in order to buy Imola. Sixtus wanted Imola as a gift to his son Girolamo Riario, whom the pope passed off as one of his numberous nephews. Because the pope already owed 10,000 florins to the Medici bank, Lorenzo hesitated, a hesitation that would cost him plenty. The pope, apoplectic, turned to the Pazzi, bankers who immediately agreed. The Pazzi were an old family with money that went way back. The manager of the Rome branch of the Pazzi bank, Francesco de' Pazzi, hated Lorenzo whom he found arrogant and far too rich for a parvenu. He hatched a plan to assassinate both Lorenzo and his brother Giuliano. For this he turned to Girolamo Riario, now lord of Imola, and Francesco Salviati, an enemy of the Medici, whom Lorenzo had forbidden to cross Florentine territory. Salviati wanted to get to Pisa where Sixtus had named him archbishop and Lorenzo's refusal to let him pass deprived him of huge sums of money. The conspirators went to get Sixtus' permission ''to take care of Lorenzo'' which the pope gave, although piously adding that he wanted no bloodshed. The conspirators then went to see Jacopo de' Pazzi, the head of the clan, who refused his consent until he was told that the pope himself had blessed the endeavor.

On the day of the planned murders, Easter Sunday, Francesco de' Pazzi went to the Medici palace in search of Giuliano who said he wouldn't be going to church because he felt ill. Giuliano was an exception among the Medici for several reasons. Although older than Lorenzo, he was never offered a position of real power by his brother. He was far handsomer than the younger Lorenzo and liked to think of himself as a woman killer, which made his entourage laugh because he lacked his brother's charm, meaning that his bed was often empty whereas Lorenzo's never lacked for company. In addition, the youths laughed behind his back because when he did find someone, far from being the heartless enslaver of women's hearts he said he was, he would fall head over heels in love, love that invariably ended with *his* heart broken. Francesco de' Pazzi was accompanied to Lorenzo's palace to fetch Giuliano by Bernardo Baroncelli, a banker and friend of both Francesco and the Medici. They persuaded Giuliano to go to church, giving him a friendly manly hug when he consented--in order to find out if he were wearing armor under his cloak.

In the cathedral Giuliano was separated from Lorenzo by a few yards. Sometime during the High Mass, thanks to a predecided signal, Baroncelli struck Giuliano with his dagger that pierced his brain. Francesco followed with more blows, twenty all together. Giuliano was dead before he hit the marble floor. Nearby two priests attached Lorenzo, one of whom nicked his neck with a dagger, but Lorenzo whipped off his cloak and held it up as protection, his sword already in his hand. As friends came to Lorenzo's aid, the attackers fled. One friend risked his life by sucking the blood oozing from Lorenzo's wound, afraid the dagger had been poisoned. Lorenzo ran to his palace, perhaps believing that his brother, whom he had not seen fall, had already returned there.

The second act of the drama took place at the Palazzo della Signoria, the Florentine Town Hall, a wonderful crenellated tower that overlooks the Piazza della Signoria and the God-inspired statue of Michelangelo's *David*. Here Salviati, the man Lorenzo had forbidden to cross Florentine land so that he could take up his position as archbishop of Pisa, led a pack of thirty mercenaries. Due to the archbishop's renown, he was allowed to enter the Palazzo della Signoria but due to his nervousness the guards felt that something was terribly amiss. The archbishop was separated from his men who were invited into a nearby chamber that one the guards immediately locked. Government officials sounded the alarm, bells that tolled in emergencies, the ringing of which automatically set in motion the ringing of other bells in other churches surrounding Florence, until the entire countryside knew that something was wrong and, in response, sent armed men to the Piazza della Signoria. The moment the guards at the Palazzo found out what had happened, they killed the thirty followers of Salviati, throwing them from the windows of the crenellated tower. Francesco was found at his palace, badly wounded by a knife blow he had inflicted on himself while stabbing Giuliano. He was taken naked to the Palazzo and hung by the neck from an upper window. Archbishop Salviati himself was flung from the same window, in full vestments. Eerily, he sank his teeth into Francesco, perhaps in revenge for getting him into such a mess, perhaps to ease the noose around his neck, perhaps due to an involuntary convulsion.

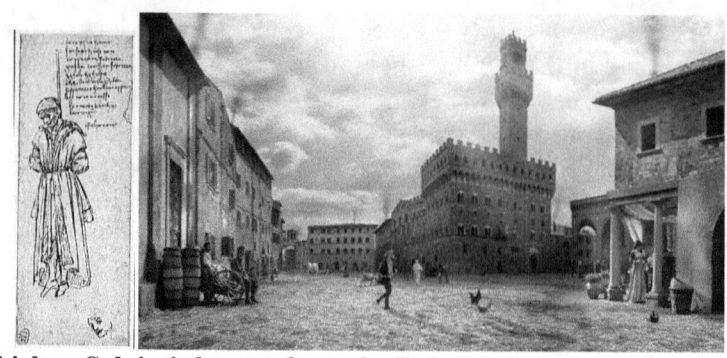

Archbishop Salviati thrown from the Palazzo della Signoria, sketch by Leonardo da Vinci.

The fifty-seven-year-old Jacopo ran for his life into the country where he was recognized by peasants, arrested, sent to a dungeon and tortured. He was then taken to the Palazzo della Signoria from whose tower he too was hurtled, dressed only in his drawers. His body was cut down and pulled through the streets of Florence by boys beating it with sticks before being nailed to the door of his palace against which they banged his head, yelling out "Open up, the master is back!" Other deaths followed, more than a hundred in all as plotters and believed plotters were hounded down.

Sixtus, sick with rage that an archbishop had been hung by the neck in his ceremonial robes, excommunicated all of Florence when the citizens refused to turn over Lorenzo to a papal court. The pope declared war on the city-state and turned to Lorenzo's dear friend, King Ferrante of Naples, for troops, which the king provided. The pope named Montefeltro, Duke of Urbino, to head the forces. Now old, the duke proved far less valorous than in times gone by. In the meantime, excommunication had put Florence in the position of a leper, cold-shouldered by its neighbors. Bands of armed youths descended on the city, robbing and raping and depriving it of food. Last rites couldn't be given and the dead couldn't be buried. Lorenzo, seeing that something extraordinary had to be done, took a ship from Pisa to Naples to appeal directly to his former friend Ferrante, a courageous move as Ferrante was as liable to cut off his head as to kiss him. Before leaving Florence Lorenzo had mortgaged his castles and palaces to raise money, money he now spent like water on making gifts to the Neapolitans, on lavish festivals and on charities. It's said, though, that although he laughed at the side of Ferrante during the day, he was in despair at night. Finally Ferrante, faced again with French desires to take Naples on the one hand and, on the other hand, confronted with Turkish ships that were approaching, freed the young man. Also thanks to the Turks, Sextus decided that he needed Florence at his side in his attempt to mount a crusade against them. He lifted the excommunication.

Lorenzo allowed the dissident monk, Savonarola, to preach in Florence where he predicted the imminent death of three dictators, Innocent VIII, Ferrante of Naples and Lorenzo himself. Both Innocent and Lorenzo died in 1492 and Ferrante, at age seventy, in 1494. Lorenzo died relatively young from complications probably due to family gout. He turned over the reins to his son Piero who immediately tried to shore up relations with Ludovico Sforza of Milan who had succeeded Galeazzo Maria Sforza. Ludovico was known to be devious and unpredictable. He had taken a liking to Lorenzo but Piero lacked his father's charm. Ludovico was in fact a regent for Galeazzo's son Gian Galeazzo, but once he'd gained power Ludovico kept it, a *fait accompli* accepted by Gian Galeazzo who preferred hunting and was considered intellectually stunted. But Gian's wife was Isabella, granddaughter of King Ferrante of Naples. Ferrante sent troops to take over Milan, forcing Ludovico to request the intervention of Charles VIII of France who considered himself the rightful possessor of Naples.

Two years after Lorenzo's death Charles entered Italy (as related earlier) at the head of 60,000 soldiers and camp followers, the greatest invasion since Hannibal. His troops, many of whom were mercenaries, were heat-tempered professions, armed with cannons and the morality of beasts. They plundered, raped and murdered their way south. Charles was quite naturally well received in Milan where, under his influence, Ludovico had Gian Galeazzo poisoned, although he spread the word that the young man had died from an excess of coitus. (Perhaps Ludovico had Charles in mind when he made the accusation against Gian Galeazzo for excessive screwing, as the French king, as reported, had several women throughout the day, and never ever the same one twice, this despite the fact that he was deemed the ugliest man alive.) Alfonso II, who had replaced Ferrante in Naples, fled the city-state. In order to protect Florence from the surge of Charles' barbarians, Piero decided to copy his father Lorenzo by going to meet Charles personally, as Lorenzo had gone to meet with Ferrante of Naples. Alas, Piero was no *Il Magnifico* and Charles, treating him with open disdain, sent him packing like a boy. At home the Signoria blamed him for all of Florence's troubles and banished him and his family, bringing down the curtain on the Medici.

In response to the terrible ravages caused by the French, the Italians finally unified in an anti-French coalition sponsored by Pope Alexander VI, noted, as said, for his unfailing courage. Venetians and Ludovico of Milan took part. Charles was forced to retreat, although in various battles the anti-French coalition lost a reported 2,000 men to every 1,000 lost by Charles. The coalition hounded the retreating French army like wolves, attacking its baggage train until nothing remained to Charles of the tons of gold, jewels and other loot he had amassed. It was two years later that Charles, on his way to a tennis match, struck his head on the lintel of a door and hemorrhaged to death. His successor, Louis XII, decided to follow up an ancient French claim to Milan by launching an attack on the city-state. Ludovico was captured by Louis and imprisoned in an underground dungeon until his death.

Savonarola had welcomed Charles with open arms to Florance, claiming that he had asked God to send the Frenchman as an arm to punish the evildoers in Italy in general, and Florence in particular. When Savonarola had first come to Florence he had gained a huge following because he had had the right answers to how Florentines could wage war against corruption, brigands and iniquity. He painted a clear picture of the depravity of the church, from the trade of indulgences to the selling of cardinal hats. He was the precursor of the coming Reformation, and because he was ahead of his time he was burned at the stake--the word of the true God gone up in flames.

That was not all that went up in flames. Ignorance and superstition took a huge hit when Ferdinand Magellan's crew circumnavigated the world, proving it was not flat. The forces that push some men to do what they do are truly mindboggling, and both Alexander VI and Magellan possessed those forces. In 1494 Alexander VI divided the world in two parts, West of a line that divided the Atlantic down the middle went to Spain, the East went to Portugal. Alexander got the king of Spain to agree to the division and, while he was at it, he gave King Ferdinand and Queen Isabella permission to initiate the Inquisition and rid Spain of Jews and Moors (it must be remembered that Alexander, a Borgia, was himself Spanish). Magellan was a totally fearless warrior, many times wounded in battles against the Arabs. Magellan set out from Seville to discover a route to the Spice Islands, the source of spices that, at the time, far outweighed gold in value. He was given five ships--all totally black due to the pitch that covered even the masts--and 260 sailors, for the most part illiterate scum who thought only of their stomachs and scrotums. They sailed first to the Canary Islands and then to Brazil. During the trip a sailor was caught sodomizing a page. Pages, aged eight to fifteen, were shanghaied to do the menial jobs onboard. The general rule at sea was simply to look away when one was caught in a sex act, the norm being that sailors, in their teens and twenties, took care of each other's carnal needs. For some unknown reason Magellan took offense now, perhaps because the boy was very young. The sailor was garroted (a rope encircled his throat and a stick--called *garrote* in Spanish--was introduced between the neck and rope and turned until the man was strangled to death). What happened to the lad is unclear. Either he jumped overboard or was thrown; at any rate, he too died. On the coast of Brazil the sailors enjoyed accepted sex with native women, the price being a nail or any other metal object. The crewmembers were careful not to venture far from the ships, as they knew that the natives practiced cannibalism and human sacrifices. The men suffered terribly from heat in summer, as well as from rats and mice that left feces and urine in their food, and lice, bedbugs and cockroaches.

The Straits of Magellan were called, at the time, the Dragon's Tail due to their horrendous complexity. To find the passage Magellan had to investigate countless dead ends. Then winter set in, terrible at this latitude: blizzards, storms, howling winds and cold so intense it was a wonder any of them survived. Magellan put the crew on half rations and because no one really believed that a passage existed and because Magellan was inflexible and unfeeling, mutiny was in the air. The first mutiny was foiled because a few crew members, loyal to Magellan, managed to trick the mutiny leader into thinking they were on his side, giving them the opportunity to grab him by the beard and plunge a dagger into both his throat and head (reported the historian Pigafetta aboard). A priest who had taken part in the revolt was abandoned, in the snow, on an island. Other traitors were mercilessly beaten but not killed as they were needed to run the ships. A few days later, under the cover of night, another ship mutinied by setting a course back to Spain. During my research I discovered an incredible quirk that existed at the time. Saints were listed as being veritable members of the crew! For example, Santo Antonio because he was known to rescue ships; Santa Barbara because she calmed storms. More incredible still, they received a percentage of the profits when the ships returned to port, profits that were turned over to the church.

When Magellan exited the straits he is said to have cried for joy. He was now in the Pacific, a stretch of water, in his mind, less in width than the Atlantic. He would discover that, in reality, it covered half the world, and he was already nearly out of food. Thanks to the Trade Winds, they made it to Guam three months later, although many men were dead from scurvy. They reached Cebu several months after that. Here Magellan became blood brothers with the Prince, both of whom mingled their blood in a bowl mixed with wine that they drank. Ravishing young girls were offered, virgins who had their vaginas enlarged from birth in order to accommodate men who inserted gold bolts through their penises, just under the glans. The tube of the bolts had a hole through which urine and semen passed. The bolted penises were difficult to insert and they didn't allow rapid movements, meaning that intercourse lasted a very long time, even an entire day, and the men could pull out only when soft. The women claimed the bolts gave them ultimate pleasure.

So friendly was Magellan with the Prince that he offered to wage the Prince's battles for him, certain of his superiority thanks to firearms. All the Prince had to do was convert to Christianity, which he did, along with 2,500 of his subjects. Magellan went after those who didn't, so numerous that their poisoned arrows and spears, aimed at the crew's unarmored legs, proved fatal to Magellan and many others.

One ship made it back to Spain, three years after having left, its sails and rigging rotting. Of the original 260 only 18 had survived, among them the ship's greatest treasure, Antonio Pigafetta, an historian who gave us such a detailed account of the voyage that books, based on his observations, have been published, from the time of his arrival to our own day.

Caterina Sforza now enters our story. That she was illegitimate was of no consequence in the Italy of the Renaissance. In that, Italy was totally exceptional. Not only was Caterina treated with the same love as her legitimate brothers and sister, she was offered the same education as the boys in the palace, unlike what girls were offered in most other parts of the country. In addition to a superb education, she learned to handle arms, to ride and to hunt. She was a Sforza, born into a family of warriors that dated back to Francisco Sforza, her grandfather. She was thusly the daughter of Francisco Sforza's son, Galeazzo Maria Sforza, whom she adored, and the mother she loved, Lucrezia Landriani. Caterina was destined to be married three times and through each of them she would proudly wear the Sforza name, Sforza meaning "force" in Italian. Her love for her father continued untainted even when, at age ten, she was betrothed to Girolamo Riario, count of Imola, who insisted on deflowering her despite the tradition that the girls should be at least fourteen. Girolamo had been offered another girl, age eleven, but her family backed out as soon as they learned of Girolamo's pedophilic tendencies. Girolamo was continuously described as depraved by contemporary historians without further details-- although the reason may simply have been his taste for virgins and a huge capacity for women in general. Caterina's wedding night may have been rough (as her father certainly knew it would be), but thereafter she was known for her numerous sexual encounters and her attraction to especially handsome lads, one of whom, a stable boy, she raised to lord of Forlì after her husband Girolamo's death. She would eventually present Girolamo with six sons and a daughter.

Girolamo was the son of a shoemaker whose good luck was to have Pope Sixtus, known for his nepotism, for uncle. Thanks to Sixtus IV Caterina became countess of Imola, that Sixtus had bought for Girolamo.

Girolamo Riario hated the Medici with every bone in his body because they had always been obstacles in every adventure initiated by the Riario. He therefore tried to assassinate Lorenzo *Il Magnifico* and his brother Giuliano, as we've seen. Girolamo would become known for his cowardliness in battle, and here too, in the attempt on Lorenzo's life, he was not to be found in the heat of things. Only the confessions of the perpetrators made it clear to all of Italy the essential role that was his in the plot. He fell into public disgrace, he infuriated his uncle Pope Sixtus, and he became the object of jokes concerning his bravery and competence. Caterina, at age sixteen, was thought to have lost trust in him.

In rapid succession she had two sons, Ottaviano, whose godfather was none other than Cardinal Rodrigo Borgia, and Cesare, named after the great Roman, he who crossed the Ribicon, a river just a short distance from Forlì.

Between Imola and Forlì was the city-state of Faenza, home of the Manfredi and birthplace of Astorre Manfredi, said to be the most beautiful boy in Italy. Imola, Forlì and Faenza were part of the Papal States, territories under the sovereign rule of the pope, and represented his temporal power on earth. Popes had only partial control over the States, some of which were under the command of one prince or another. The hold over Faenza by the Mandredi was backed by the Este family of Ferrara, a country to the north of Faenza, too powerful for the current pope to bring into the Papal States. The power in Forlì, on the other hand, had gone from despot to pope and back again for centuries. At the moment it was in the hands of the Ordelaffi.

Antonio Ordelaffi had come to power in Forlì thanks to Venice. Forlì was a well-fortified city surrounded by walls and surmounted by the nearby fortress of Ravaldino that controlled passage between the north and south of Italy, as well as roads entering the Apennines. The city was passed on to Antonio's son Francesco who was murdered by his brother Pino. Pino failed to take Machiavelli's advice in such cases, he exiled Francesco's small sons instead of strangling them as did the Turks their brothers and brothers' sons. Pino then went on to poison his wife whom he suspected of infidelity. As she had been born in neighboring Faenza, he gained the enmity of the Manfredi. The next to be poisoned was his second wife and his second wife's mother, both from Imola, gaining him the hatred of the Imolesi. Pino's third bride, Lucrezia Mirandola, was said to carefully watch what she ate. He had no children from any of his wives but did produce a bastard whom he named to succeed him when he fell ill. So hated was he by even his own Forlivesi that he was pulled from his sick bed and dragged through the city streets, spat upon and kicked until he was unrecognizable.

His wife Lucrezia became regent for Pino's son but Francesco's boys, now youths, returned to take power. They easily took the city but not the adjoining fortress, Ravaldino, a fortress that would play an important part, later, in the story of Caterina Riario Sforza de' Medici herself. It was within Ravaldino that Lucrezia and her son took refuge. But the boy mysteriously died, giving Pope Sixtus IV the excuse he needed to send in Caterina's husband Girolamo. Girolamo's army chased the three youths from Forlì and now both Forlì and Imola belonged to him and Caterina, count and countess, but not the fortress of Ravaldino. Because it was unbreachable, Pope Sixus offered Lucrezia 139,000 ducats and a new castle if she would leave, which she gladly did.

Caterina and Girolamo visited their new acquisition, a backwater in comparison to Rome (which was, compared to Florence, a slum). The inhabitants were awed by the noble dress of the royal couple, their beautiful horses, the trumpets, flags, banners and pennants.

Now all the count needed was the city-state lying between Forlì and Imola: Faenza. Famous for its ceramics (faience, ergo the name Faenza) and bricks (from which Ravaldino was constructed), it was a land of vineyards and fertile valleys. At the moment Faenza was ruled by Galeotto Manfredi who had the support of his neighbor to the north, Ferrara, ruled by Ercole d'Este. Galeotto's wife was also the daughter of the lord of Bologna. Although Ferrara was powerful and Ercole a condottiere, the powers of the region were clearly Milan, Florence, Venice and Bologna. Ercole was hated by the pope and by Girolamo because of his support of Florence and Lorenzo *Il Magnifico*. As Lorenzo would have been glad to stick a dagger into Girolamo's throat because of his role in Lorenzo's brother's death, Galeotto Manfredi benefited from extremely serious assistance. Girolamo and his only support, Sixtus IV, had to renounce, for the time being, the seizure of Faenza.

To change air, Caterina decided to visit her mother, sister and relatives in Milan. There, to her stupefaction, she found a city in full bloom thanks to Ludovico Sforza who, against all preconceived notions, had opened Milan to engineers, architects and artists. In fact, the city was being rebuild from the foundations up. The most famous Sforza acquisition was the young Leonardo da Vince whom everyone found gorgeous--slim, strong, physically powerful and possessing cascades of hair flowing around his beautiful face. Caterina anticipated a close relationship by offering the boy a commission to do her portrait. Alas for her, this boy preferred other boys.

Back home in Forlì, Caterina became more and more aware of her husband's unpopularity. Then things boiled over, and what Caterina had expected finally happened. One of the noble clans, the Orsi, had had enough of Girolamo. As close friends of his, they were allowed to enter the palace early one afternoon while Girolamo was resting, and knifed him. Girolamo was able to raise himself and attempted to get to Caterina's rooms but the Orsi brothers kept slashing with daggers until he lay in a pool of his own blood. The body was thrown over the balcony into the piazza where Forlivesi examined the mangled remains and bloody face. At first fearful, they turned on it once they knew the tyrant was truly dead. He was kicked, spat upon and beaten. The Forlivesi then sacked the palace, taking away everything, down to the bedding. The Orsi ran to Caterina's apartments where she was entertaining her mother, sister and children. The children broke into terrified sobs, only Girolamo's bastard son, Scipione, age fourteen, faced the attackers with bravado. They were all locked in but luckily Caterina was able to get a message out to Naples and Bologna, as well as to the new pope, Innocent VIII in Rome. Bishop Savelli, who happened to be touring the region, entered Forlì the next day and immediately, on learning what was going on, went to make sure that nothing had happened to Caterina and her children. As the population knew that she could count on the huge armies of both Milan and Bologna, neither it nor the Orsi dared harm her. In addition, the mighty fortification of Ravaldino was in the hands of a man loyal to the countess.

Whether Bishop Savelli was in league with Caterina or not is unknown. What is known is that he accompanied her to the fortification of Ravaldino that she promised to hand over to the Orsi. The keeper, in league with her, said he would do so if she would pay his back wages and ensure his future employment there or elsewhere. When she agreed, he said she would have to enter the fortification and give him what he wanted in writing. The Orsi rejected the idea until Bishop Savelli vouched for her integrity. She entered Ravaldino, the door closed behind her, she mounted the steps to the top of the tower where she gave the Orsi--the finger.

The Orsi, outraged, went back to the palace where they fetched her oldest son Ottaviano, age nine. He was brought back before the walls of Ravaldino and a dagger was placed against the lad's throat, the worst possible nightmare for a mother. The child was obliged to cry out for mercy, alerting Caterina to his presence. She returned to the top of the tower and stared down at the Orsi, their troops and the town people who had desecrated the body of her husband and ransacked her palace. She felt she had little to fear as they were all deathly afraid of the consequences of their acts. Spies had already returned to Forlì to inform them that troops from Bologna and Milan were on the way, and they all knew too that the new pope would never accept that even a hair of any of the children be harmed. Accordingly, Caterina hollered out the words that have made her famous to this day. She told them all that they could do what they would with her children as she was pregnant again and with *this*, she added, pointing to her loins, she could produce many others.

Caterina's stance at Ravaldino had a highly unforeseeable consequence. Antonio Maria Ordelaffi, whose family Girolamo had chased from Forlì when he took power, had two messages sent to Caterina by arrows shot over the walls of Ravaldino, both suggesting that she and he marry. As the boy was young and handsome, he would soon gain access to her. But for the moment, 12,000 Milanese soldiers arrived to save Caterina. The troops were prepared for battle and for the inevitable sacking of Forlì, their reward. Seeing them, the Orsi brothers hurried to put their threat in action before being forced to flee: they went to kill the Girolamo children. Happily, the children had been hidden away by Bishop Savelli, whose presence had truly been a godsend. The Forlivesi had a sudden change of heart. They now cried out "Ottaviano!," the name of Girolamo's heir, the boy who had nearly had his throat slit. The lad was brought to them, totally mystified by the events that he had in no way been responsible for, and was paraded around the main square of the city three times, symbolizing that he was now accepted as the new lord of Forlì.

When Caterina had regained control, she coolly dismissed the thousands of soldiers who had come to her rescue and were waiting to enter and ransack the city. Soldiers always earned part of their pay thusly, an accepted practice recognized by everyone. But Caterina told them, with mind-boggling dispassion and courage, that as the Forlì had stolen everything she possessed, what the soldiers would take in sacking the city belonged, in reality, to her. More incredible still, the soldiers let her get away with it. As for the Orsi, they left Forlì in search of asylum elsewhere and historically simply vanished from the face of the earth. They left their father behind, however, who, at age eighty, was dragged from his bed cursing his sons *for not having succeeded*! His palace was torn down and the old man pulled through the streets tied upside down to the back of a horse, his head smashed to a pulp against the cobblestones.

In neighboring Faenza its ruler Galeotto was murdered by his wife. Just being married and having children was normally sufficient for a woman during the Renaissance; a wife's husband's extramarital indiscretions were his business. Women were watched over and chastity belts really existed, especially in Florence, to keep women from unlawful intercourse and from pleasuring themselves. But Francesca Bentivoglio, Galeotto's wife, was an exceptional woman whose father just happened to be the ruler of Bologna. Her rival was a beauty known as the Peacock, whom Galeotto was rumored to have secretly married before meeting Francesca, making him a bigamist. Francesca's father knew about the affair and tried to get his son-in-law to mend his ways but failed. When Francesca finally discovered the truth, she fled home, certain that Galeotto would poison her. Through the good offices of Lorenzo *Il Magnifico*, she returned to Galeotto, but only to have him assassinated. The murder was slapsticks comedy, with three assassins hiding under the bed and one behind the bedroom door. In the ensuing struggle it was purportedly Francesca who delivered the decisive blow, a dagger plunged into her husband's chest. But before dying Galeotto had done at least one thing right, he had fathered Astorre Manfredi who was, as I said, the most beautiful boy in Italy.

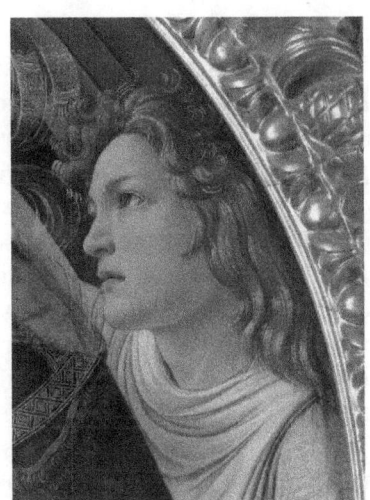

Thought to be Astorre Manfredi

Antonio Maria Ordelaffi, who was both young and handsome and had gained access to Caterina thanks to the messages shot over the walls of Ravaldino by arrow, immediately offered Francesca his hand in marriage, Bologna being infinitely more desirable than Forlì. Bologna laughed at the offer but decided that with Galeotto dead it was the perfect time for it and Milan to send troops to bring Faenza over to their sides. Lorenzo *Il Magnifico*, although an ally of Milan, didn't want the Milanese to extend their control so far to the south. Lorenzo lacked troops but not intelligence. He spread rumors about Faenza being sacked by the troops from Bologna and Milan, the troops outside of Forlì, the troops that Caterina had prevented from entering her town. They were now ready to descend on Faenza, said Lorenzo, rousing the inhabitants into action. The outcome was chaos that Pope Innocent VIII ended by issuing an edict, in 1488, confirming three-year-old Astorre Manfredi as lord of Faenza and named an eight-member regency of noble citizens to care for the lad and the city-state. The boy had now embarked on the world stage. His mother, Francesca the assassin, remained safely in Bologna. At the same time that little Astorre was made prince of Faenza, the child Ottaviano was confirmed as ruler of Imola and Forlì, under the regency of Caterina.

Humanism played a great part in the education of the young Astorre. It consisted of classical authors, especially Cicero, and included studies in philosophy, history, rhetoric, grammar, mathematics, poetry, music and astronomy. Based on the Greek ideal of a sound mind in a sound body, it included also archery, dance and swimming. There was hunting, which boys took to naturally. Humanists insisted on the genius of man, on morality and on the extraordinary potential of the human mind. Schooling was for rich boys but places were available for poor students of recognized ability. A model education combined the classics with the basics of Christianity. Once a boy developed himself intellectually and physically, he was in the ideal position to become an ideal man, as well as having prepared himself for the best possible afterlife. Latin as well as Tuscan vernacular were in usage. Dante wrote his works in Tuscan Italian, as did the wonderful Boccaccio. One of Caterina's lovers, Pietro Bembo, helped establish Tuscan Italian as the language of the entire peninsula.

Erasmus was named the Prince of Humanists. Before the arrival of humanism men believed in eternal salvation after death, but philosophers such as Erasmus preached the enrichment of life in the here and now. According to him, the church had to free itself of superstitious and corrupt behavior. It had to drop its pomp, relics and beads used as magical charms. Cults based on saints and indulgences, the purpose of which was to make money by reducing the time believers would spend in hell, had to be proscribed. (One priest was fond of telling people that as soon as a coin rings in the bowl, the soul for whom it is paid will fly out of purgatory and wing straight to heaven.) He fiercely believed in free will, without which human moral action would have no meaning. He accused monks, priests and popes of living in luxury after taking vows of poverty, of caring for their own needs before those of their flocks. Life began in the womb, he wrote, and one shouldn't be baptized until old enough to accept Christ. He believed that lust was a natural body function like the need to eat. He denounced those who waged war as beasts and he pitied the stupidity, ignorance and gullibility of the ''faithful''. Erasmus favored circumcision. (He would have been better off letting boys decide for themselves, after puberty, as he did for baptisms.) While on penis-related subjects, I can add that he is idealized by gay groups for being homosexual; heteros furiously deny it. This reminds me of those historians who believe that the Borgia should rot in hell for their iniquity, while others make a saint of Alexander VI. The truth, naturally, is that no one will ever be certain one way or another about either Erasmus or Alexander.

Thanks to Gutenberg's press, Erasmus' books were known far and wide. Nearly 4,000 pages could be produced by movable type per week compared to several pages that were hand copied. Erasmus could thusly publish thousands of copies of his books, making him a best seller (750,000 of his works were sold during his lifetime alone). The advance was due to three factors: the use of the screw press, known since antiquity and used for crushing grapes and olives; the invention of metal type, in this case finding a perfect alloy consisting of lead, tin and antimony (which gives type its hardness); and the proper ink, which was oil based, more durable than water based. Gutenberg's press played a key role in the dissemination of knowledge to the masses, breaking forever the monopoly of literacy held by the nobles. By year 1500 there were 77 cities throughout Italy that had printing shops.

Erasmus formed a long friendship with Thomas More, a supposed humanist whose reputation was considerably muddied by the six executions for heresy during his chancellorship. More was against the Reformation which cost him his life under Henry VIII who died in his bed in terrible pain, small retribution for the thousands of woman, boys and men he'd had hanged for one reason or another.

It's of interest to know what else was going on in the world at this time, a time especially harsh on boys. In 1485 the English king Richard III gave orders for his two nephews, Edward V (who had just been crowned king), age 13, and his brother, Richard Duke of York, age 9, to be smothered to death in the Tower of London. According to Alison Weir's wonderful book *The Princes in the Tower*, the boys certainly suspected what awaited them, as they had grown increasingly melancholy. Then, suddenly, they ceased appearing at the windows of their chambers. Richard III was given a summary burial at his death, due to his role in the murders, and has been despised throughout history ever since, giving both Shakespeare and Sir Lawrence Olivier moments of creative glory. There can be no more heinous crime than the killing of children, and what awaited Astorre and his brother was even worse as they had marks of torture on their bodies, and both were said to have been abused sexually before being thrown into the Tiber.

Nothing illustrates better the harshness of treatment reserved for boys as does *The Sacrifice of Isaac*, the cover picture of this book.

Again, one can only tremble before Caravaggio's brilliance. A painting so perfect that one's throat contracts, on the edge of vomiting at the outrage of a father on the verge of slitting his own son's throat, all due to the belief in a vengeful god who tries his servant Abraham's loyalty, the same obscurantism we find in the three major western religions that have historically caused the death of countless thousands--and continue to do so-- all because we are still ruled by the reptilian segment of the brain that bends before fear and superstition and ignorance, that refuses our taking responsibility for our own acts. An afterlife at the feet of Christ, or in bed with 72 virgins, or post-birth mutilation through circumcision. The horror of such a black hole is herein represented by a father who would slit the throat of his precious boy, all for the chimerical belief in an ethereal heaven.

Even if the angel does still Abraham's knife, the boy has been traumatized beyond endurance and the genius of Caravaggio is to portray the absolute horror in the boy's face, a boy terrified, a boy paralyzed with fear, his body held down by the weight of his father, his father's hand clamped over his neck, his thumb driven into the boy's cheek. How many other lads have been terrified in this way throughout the ages, threatened by men like Abraham, their necks cut open, a bullet lodged in their heads, their hearts, still beating, extracted by the thousands to ensure that the sun would rise again? Like the mindless miscreants who wish for us to discover other planets because we are incapable of caring for the wondrous one we already have, men like Abraham wage war here and now while promising greener pastures elsewhere. Personally I think I'll regret this earth, but I won't regret the inhumanity that rules it.

Such is the stirring power of Caravaggio's *The Sacrifice of Isaac*. The boy, by the way, was Cecco.

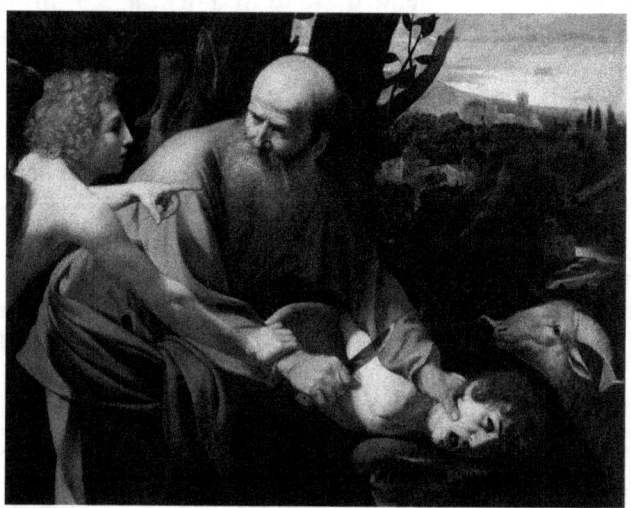

The Sacrifice of Isaac

Despite the fact that Cesare had murdered his brother and Alexander's favorite son, Juan, both father and the remaining son, Cesare, now formed a tandem (it is difficult to count the insignificant Jofrè), the purpose of which was to extend Alexander's power and to give Cesare enough strength so that he would be able to replace the pope, at his death, becoming the first ruler of a unified Italy since the Romans.

To get things going, Alexander arranged a rapprochement between Louis XII of France and the Vatican. This the pope accomplished thanks to three of the new king's needs: the need to conquer Milan; the need to reconquer Naples, lost with the death of Charles VIII; and the need for a divorce so that Louis could marry Charles' widow. Louis offered Alexander a huge sum of money and gave Cesare, whom all recognized as the new rising star, the duchy of Valence. Cesare would also be given command over several thousand French troops. Satisfied, Alexander threw in a cardinal's hat that the French had requested for years. Not to be outdone, Louis raised the stakes by offering to find Cesare a noble wife.

When Cesare realized that he would soon be meeting Louis in person, he decided to turn himself into a perfect male by force of exercise, physical exercise as well as exercise in arms and horsemanship. He spent hours at the task and contemporaries agreed that there was not a finer looking Italian in all of Italy, with the exception of Astorre Manfredi who began to draw artists and sculptures to Faenza to capture his face for eternity. The artists who flocked to do Astorre honor wielded an art that was reborn, one that took its roots in humanism and in classical antiquity. It was based on classical texts rediscovered thanks to the likes of Cosimo de' Medici and thanks to commissions by the powerful Julius II. It was accompanied by technical advances that improved the quality of oil paint adopted by Titian, Tintoretto and Uccello. Da Vinci perfected the art of painting thanks to lighting and perspective, as well as incredible detail in anatomy and landscape.

Cesare's face may not have equaled the beauty of Astorre's, but his good looks were increasingly disfigured by the ravages of syphilis. The syphilitic rashes, euphemistically called ''flowers'', came and went like the tide, leaving him handsome or disfigured *selon*. He took to wearing masks during his bad days, the effect of which enhanced the fear people already had of him.

When the time came, Cesare set off for France with cartloads of precious gifts. He was beautifully dressed in black and white velvet, pearls and gold chains and precious gems attached to his clothes and boots, his horse was attired in gorgeous livery and silver bells. In addition, he had not forgotten the cardinal's hat to be presented to Georges d'Amboise, Louis' trusted counselor. Cesare was offered the sister of the King of Navarre, sixteen-year-old Carlotta. Louis wrote Alexander a description of the wedding night, telling the pope that Cesare honored his wife eight times in a row. Louis added that he had done the same with his new wife--thanks to the divorce Alexander had accorded him--but confessed that he had nonetheless done less well as his sessions had been broken up, twice before dinner, six times afterwards. Alexander replied that he was awed by the king and proud of his son but not surprised by his virility. Carlotta was immediately pregnant. Charles' former wife wasn't.

As Louis XII's troops descended into Italy, Ludovico Sforza fled Milan with all the booty he could carry and Frederico did the same in Naples, choosing the island of Ischia for his exile. Ludovico was later captured by the French and spent the remaining years of his life in prison, Frederico was awarded a pension and died in the French town of Tours.

Now that Alexander and Cesare were aligned with France against Milan and Naples, Lucrezia's new husband Alfonso, illegitimate son of the former king of Naples Alfonso II, was an embarrassment that the two men eliminated by eliminating Alfonso himself. The boy had dined with the pope and was on his way home when waylaid by men with daggers. Wounded, he was taken to the Vatican where the pope gave him his own rooms. Instinctively knowing what was in store for the lad she loved, Lucrezia hovered over him day and night. Alfonso knew who was responsible for his injuries, and when he had recuperated enough, he took a potshot at Cesare with a crossbow as he passed through the garden below Alfonso's window. Cesare was unscathed, but his reaction was immediate. He sent men to clear Alfonso's rooms of both Alfonso's sister, Sancia, and his wife, Lucrezia. When they refused to budge, the men told the women that they were acting under orders from the pope himself. If the two women doubted their word they could ask the pope who was in an adjoining apartment. As they left to do so, the doors to Alfonso's rooms were closed and Alfonso strangled. Cesare made no pretense of innocence, maintaining that since Alfonso had tried to kill him, he was only protecting his life.

Cesare then left Rome at the head of thousands of French troops and headed for the Romagna and the city-states he was set on conquering in the name of the pope because they were, after all, Papal States. On his way he visited his dear sister Lucrezia who was recuperating at Nepi after the loss of her beloved Alfonso. One wonders what they had to say to each other....

One of the men accompanying Cesare was the artist Pietro Torrigiano. His story is singular because Torrigiano was a sculptor under the patronage of Lorenzo *Il Magnifico*. He is credited with bringing the artistic segment of the Renaissance to England where he finished out his life. But through a quirk of human nature, he is known today as the man who broke the nose of Michelangelo. Torrigiano had been one of Michelangelo's lovers and, in a fit of jealousy, smashed the great artist in the face. Knowing how furious Lorenzo would be at his disfiguring Michelangelo, Torrigiano fled. As Cesare was offering money to new conscripts, and as Torrigiano needed money, he joined his troops. Later he would become renown for sculpting the memorial to Henry VII of England, a man as atypical as Torrigiano.

From Nepi Cesare went on to Rimini to capture the city-state from the Malatesta. The Malatesta were a family of hotheads, schemers and murderers who ruled Rimini from 1295 until the arrival of Cesare who extinguished them with the ease of blowing out a candle. The first Malatesta was a hunchback, Giovanni, who killed his wife Francesce and his brother Paolo when he discovered them in flagrante delicto.

The Malatesta were often condottieri in the service of other Italian city-states. The most famous was Sigismondo. He took up arms at age 13 and became lord of Rimini at 15. He murdered his first wife and was known for his treason, first against the pope, then against the Sforza, the Florentines and finally the Neapolitans. After drowning his second wife he succeeded in betraying Siena, Venice, the Sforza for a second time and Florence again. Pope Pius excommunicated him for acts of sodomy on his own son. He was also accused of incest with his daughters, also par for the course during the period. Most of the above city-states raised troops to get rid of him, under the direction of Federico da Montefeltro. He fled to Venice where the Serenissima, who never did anything like the others, took him in. He plotted to assassinate the pope but returned home instead to peacefully die in his bed.

On his way back from Rimini Cesare came upon the sister of the ruler of Rimini whom he had just chased from power, the grandson of Sigismondo. Cesare immediately sequestered and raped her over a period of months, denying any knowledge of her whereabouts. Anyway, he scoffed, he didn't need to rape women as they came to him willingly from everywhere. Which was true. Ambassadors from many city-states were nonetheless so upset by the abduction that they joined forces in demanding that Alexander severely punish his son. Alexander too was reported as being upset, but in the end, what could he do? The woman was eventually restored to her husband but from what she reported later, either she was suffering from Stockholm syndrome or her months with Cesare hadn't been all that traumatizing.

The time had come for Lucrezia to marry again, a marriage which would, naturally, benefit the pope. Alexander thusly chose the son of Duke Ercole of Ferrara, another Alfonso, Alfonso d'Este, for his daughter Lucrezia. Behind closed doors the Duke of Ferrara laughed at such pretention. His family was noble, old and wealthy, that of Alexander hick parvenus. Ercole had heard stories about them all, that Alexander had prostitutes from the best bordellos brought to him after dinner, that Cesare slept during the day and whored at night, that both he and his dad had shared Lucrezia, that they were murderous slime, socially nonexistent and morally rotten to the core.

Yet … his own boy was perhaps little better. Alfonso was known to have two interests in life, making cannons in his own personal foundry and parading around town at night, his sword in one hand, his erect cock in the other. His former wife had been so fed up with him that she turned to women for satisfaction. Stories of incest, sodomy, rape, murder, *et j'en passe* may seem exaggerated, but personally I believe they represent just the tip of the iceberg. The repressive atmosphere during the deep darkness that followed the fall of Imperial Rome was such that when the light finally came, when the period known as the Renaissance finally rose from ancient Rome's ashes, the liberation--intellectual, artistic and sexual--was such that Italy knew few bounds. And this liberation came to a people that just happened to be among the most beautiful created by the fertile mind of God.

But the wedding did take place since Louis XII of France wanted it, all because he needed the Borgias to further his ambitions. The price Ercoli demanded would have been dismissed out of hand by any other person in Italy, but not Alexander who disposed of literally bottomless resources, resources brought in, in multiple ways, every single day, via every church in the country. Alfonse was 26, Lucrezia still only 21. Parties were thrown in Rome prior to her leaving the city, one of which, in 1501, was the famous Banquet of the Chestnuts already described, during which prizes were given to those who could come the most times and copulate with the most prostitutes. Some say Lucrezia was present. Some put Cesare there. Others, place them both. All named Alexander.

The trip to Ferrara and the celebration there cost a fortune, but the wedding night came off well. Alexander was told that Alfonso had contented Lucrezia that night and then took his pleasure with other women during the day. The pope supposedly thought this just fine as Alfonso was a young man and, as such, multiple adventures were good for him. The historian Burchard wrote that all the talk of lubricity inspired the pope to increase the number of prostitutes he welcomed into his rooms that night. As always in Italy, love was indeed in the air.

In Forlì love was also in the air. Caterina decided to see Antonio Maria Ordelaffi. Their relationship lasted months, during which the Forlivesi happily anticipated the coming marriage. After all, Caterina, decided and intelligent as she was, was nonetheless a woman and as such needed male direction. (No matter what she accomplished, the idea that she depended on men would hold true until her death.) But Caterina had other ideas. She had had her eye on a stable boy, Giacomo Feo, since he was fifteen. Now seventeen, tall, lithe and supranormally handsome, his contemporaries tell us he was big where it counted. When Caterina found herself pregnant, she secretly married the kid.

All hell broke out in every direction. Forlivesi and Imolesi couldn't accept the primacy of a stable boy over their cities, and Bologna, Milan, Florence and Ferrara proclaimed that they had youths of noble birth who could satisfy the countess at least as much as Feo. The city that eventually won out, should Caterina choose one of their boys, would not only broaden its territory thanks to its influence over the two city-states, but it would control a major artery through the Apennines. Foiled attempts were made on the lives of both the countess and her lad, but she brought her pregnancy to term, giving birth to a baby boy, Bernardino. The marriage and the baby were kept secret because she did not want to undermine the ascension of Girolamo's son Ottaviano. She thusly decided to end any rumors concerning one or the other by punishing the rumormongers. She had them systematically beaten, many of whom were permanently maimed and at least one was killed. But it was a wonderful period for Caterina. A visiting ambassador was allowed into the inner sanctum of Caterina's palace where she and Giacomo were playing with Catherina's children by Girolamo and her son by Feo. He described the husband and wife, in the light of the setting sun, as pure angels.

It was now 1495 and her son Ottaviano, age 16, was a man. In an attempt to gain what was his, he went up to his mother and Feo and demanded to be recognized as the new count of Forlì and Imola. An argument ensued that ended with Feo slapping the boy who stormed out of the room red-faced. A week later, as Feo was riding through the woods along with Caterina, a group of friends approached them on horse. As Feo chatted amiably with one, another stuck a dagger in his back. Caterina had the presence of mind to turn and ride off to the impregnable shelter of Ravaldino. Feo's bodyguards also took flight, leaving the handsome boy to fall from his horse into a ditch.

The people of Forlì remembered the heads Caterina ordered cut off after the assassination of Girolama. So when the murderers of Feo came riding into the town square, their clothes filthy with his blood, shouting to all the account of their exploits which, they maintained, were designed to give power over Forlì and Imola to their rightful count, Ottaviano, a group of nobles thought best to go to Ravaldino to find out what had really happened. When they returned, they ordered the arrest of the assassins. The reprisals were indeed terrible. The murderers had their heads axed open, from the top to the chin. Their wives and mistresses and children were slaughtered. Their houses were torn down brick by brick. Two babies associated with them, age three and nine months, along with their nurses, were bludgeoned to death. An accused priest was dragged behind a horse, his head fractured against the cobblestones, as Caterina had ordered done to Girolamo's assassin, old man Orsi. Under torture another conspirator gave out the name of her son Ottaviano, known by all to have hated Feo for usurping his rightful place as count of Forlì and Imola. Caterina had her son arrested, an act so horrifying that the inhabitants followed the boy to the gates of Ravaldino where Caterina dispersed them with cannon fire. After a stormy meeting with his mother, the boy was put under house arrest. At Feo's funeral all of Forlì and Imola turned out, so afraid were the populations of their countess. Heaven entered the act by bringing down a plague on the people: rashes appeared on their genitals and their lymph nodes swelled up. The syphilis epidemic had begun. Caterina ordered her palace torn down because it had sheltered both her and Feo, and his statue in bronze was raised in his honor. A new palace was build on the grounds of fortified Ravaldino. Its furnishings and gardens were so exquisite that Caterina called the place Paradise. She sent Ottaviano to Florence to learn the art of war. The sixteen-year-old lad, a veritable Don Juan like his father Girolamo, left behind mistresses and bastards.

Caterina had eight children. Bianca Riario was her only girl and Caterina destined her for the handsome Astorre Manfredi of neighboring Faenza. All the surrounding powers had their say in the matter, some for and some against, but the negatives and positives equaled themselves out. For Caterina the union of the lad, age ten, and the lass, age fourteen, would unify the region, as Faenza was exactly in the middle between Forlì and Imola. Faenza was ruled by a Council which was doing an excellent job of both educating the young Astorre and of governing the tiny city-state. A pretender, however, Ottaviano Manfredi, Astorre's cousin, decided that the time was ripe for him to take power from the boy who was still a child. The resulting disorder attracted the attention of Venice who was always on the lookout for an easy kill. Bologna came to the same conclusion, as did Milan. All three decided to descend on Faenza. The brouhaha dissuaded Caterina from pursuing the marriage with Astorre and it was therefore annulled. Bianca would finally find a suitor, a count from the region of Parma, when she attained the ripe old age of twenty-two.

For Caterina, marital bliss occurred much sooner. At age thirty-three she fell in love with Giovanni de' Medici, thirty, perhaps the first veritably educated man in her life, who was also handsome and charming and, said one wag, a boy for whom she would kill father and mother to keep near her. They were secretly married because of Ludovico of Milan's enmity towards Florence. Knowing that he would find out anyway, Caterina tried to soothe Ludovico's anger by naming her only child with Giovanni, Ludovico Sforza de' Medici. Incredibly, her new husband Giovanni had inherited, in spades, the ills of his ancestors: he died in Caterina's arms, probably of complications due to family gout. In his memory she renamed her child Giovanni Sforza de' Medici.

That Caterina's private life was in shambles didn't mean she couldn't try to find happiness for her children. So when Alexander VI, her son Ottaviano's godfather, suggested a marriage between the boy and Lucrezia, Alexander's daughter, she knew that this would be the first step in turning over Forlì and Imola to the pope. Such a marriage could also turn out to be disastrous for her boy, Ottaviano. Caterina remembered that Lucrezia's first husband had been declared impotent after three years of marriage despite the boy's outcry that he'd had her ''at least a thousand times,'' and the fact too that he'd fathered bastards. So to protect her boy Caterina refused Alexander's offer, and in the nick of time too. The next candidate, Alfonso, was strangled on Cesare's orders.

Alexander decided on the direct approach and sent Cesare to bring Forlì and Imola into the lap of the Papal States. Caterina put the finishing touches on the defenses of Ravaldino just as Cesare arrived at the head of an army of twelve thousand of Louis XII's French troops. After promising her money and a palace of her own in Rome, the tone between the two-- Cesare on his white charger facing the drawbridge to Ravaldino, Caterine atop the crenellated tower--turned sour as one insulted the other. They split up but after a few hours of reflection Cesare returned. This time Caterina was standing on the drawbridge. Cesare dismounted and approached the edge. Luckily for him, he was in beauty that day. The terrible traces of his syphilis had temporarily disappeared. Handsome and gorgeously dressed in black velvet, a rarity during the period when both sexes preferred bright colors (after the austerity of the Middle Ages), he decided to trade the filthy language he was partial to with the troops (similar to today when, in the locker room, it is impossible to hear a single sentence without the obligatory insertion of fuck) for the sparkling oratory of the likes of Cicero. Caterina too was in beauty, her breasts propped up by a tight bodice. She was immediately aware that Cesare had come to seduce her with a stunning smile similar to that used by Stanley Kowalski to mollify his wife Stella. Caterina, with the same intention, turned a welcoming shoulder in his direction, he held out a hand to touch it, she enticingly took a step back in the direction of the door to Ravaldino, he followed ... until he felt the drawbridge rising under his feet. He jumped off just in time to see Caterina disappear behind the closing door. Cesare, his face red with shame for having been tricked, stormed off.

Sadly, Cesare would win out. What Caterina had pointed to when the Orsi had put a dagger against the throat of her son when ordering her to surrender Ravaldino, what one contemporary had referred to as her "cunt" in a letter, would soon be not only his, but his until he himself felt that his humiliation of her had gone on long enough. (Although some writers during the period suggested that she grew to *like* Cesare and his form of humiliation. Naturally, we'll never ever know.)

At any rate, Cesare immediately went back to his obscene military language and ordered an all-out attack on the citadel. I won't go into the actual destruction except to say that she was betrayed from inside the walls, walls opened to Cesare and his French troops. The Italians inside were spared but ransomed; the mercenaries under Caterina had their throats slit. She stepped over seven hundred strewn corpses on her way out of Ravaldino, in time to see her monument of bronze to her beloved Feo being carted away prior to being melted into cannon balls. Feo was symptomatic of what had undermined her place in Forlì and Imola: she had fought for her own pleasure and a place in the sun for her children; she had known lads and wealth and luxury beyond measure; and so as one citizen summed it all up as she was hauled away, "She had put her faith in herself and in the walls of her fortress, and none in the people she ruled".

The French commanders observed the fate of the women left behind, their thighs spread as the men lined up. They knew that the prettiest had already been put aside for themselves later on. Realizing what was in store for Caterina, several tried to save the countess by telling Cesare that they had precedence over her and would assure her safety right up to the moment she came before King Louis XII. This hiatus ended in an exchange of money. Cesare retired with the countess while the French officers, rich, sought the comfort of the naked forms awaiting them under the covers of their own beds. One of them was heard to say, as he unbuttoned his superb military tunic, "Well, at least she won't be wanting for fucking."

As with all seventeen-year-olds, Astorre Manfredi had everything to live for. Of medium height, with a boyish chest and slim waist, his eyes were blue and his hair as blond as gold--curly waves of which descended to his shoulders. He was courteous, had a good word for everyone, and was as aware of his charm and sexual appeal as is every Italian boy, then as today. His family had ruled the city-state of Faenza for two centuries, and although there had been some bad apples, the Manfredi, in general, had done somewhat better than the other lords, dukes and princes of the Romagna. Astorre himself was loved. Although the real power behind Faenza lay with the Council that had been regent since Astorre Manfredi was named lord at age three, he had his word to say and that word was listened to more and more frequently. Faenza was one of the few veritable free spirits to exist outside Florence, and it was more of a Republic than even the Florentine city.

Indeed, Astorre had everything to live for, and perhaps even a bit more as he had received the best education available. Private tutors had instructed him in Latin, even if his daily speech was in the Italian vernacular. He had read Homer and Plato, the Greek tragedians, Suetonius and Xenophon and Plutarch, he had studied the texts of Cicero and was himself on the road to becoming an accomplished speaker.

Puberty had come later than it does today, but he had already known girls and women. In fact, his extreme beauty brought blushes to the maidens in the market. His marriage to Caterina's daughter Bianca had fallen through but it was of little consequence as there were plenty of other matches to be made with girls from far more important towns than were Forlì and Imola.

Faenza was well fortified, but its strategic location meant it was in continual danger from this power or that. Like the threat of the atomic bomb today, Faenza, being surrounded by powers such as Bologna, Milan, Florence and Venice, was in a strategic position because if one power dared to attack, the others would tear it to pieces in order to maintain the status quo. Faenza was fortified, but with Cesare prowling around the region the citizens of the city-state decided to add to their fortifications and ensure that neighboring cities would come to their succor if and when needed.

Astorre's first appeal for support went to neighboring Bologna. After all, his mother was the sister of Giovanni Bentivoglio, the lord of Bologna. Bentivoglio sent a thousand troops to Faenza but was later forced to withdraw them due to pressure from the French king Louis XII and also the pope who threatened excommunication. Louis thanked Bentivoglio for the withdrawal by taking Bologna under his wing, thus preserving the city from future ravages by Cesare. The pope also sent a note of thanks. As a sign of further capitulation, Bentivoglio agreed to feed and house a number of Louis and Cesare's soldiers. Astorre appealed to Venice, a power he could usually depend upon, but Venice too was afraid of Louis and besides, when Louis overran Milan he gave certain lands adjoining Venice to the Serenissima who was now in his debt.

When Cesare did more than prowl, when he attacked and ravaged neighboring Forlì and Imola, Faenzans were armed and readied for action. At first Cesare tried charm. He met with the Council and with Astorre, informing them that the time had come for Faenza--like Forlì and Imola--to return to the lap of the Papal States under the direction of their pope, Alexander VI. Nothing would change other than papal troops being stationed in the fort, in addition to Faenzans being enrolled in the ever-more-numerous papal armies. Astorre and the Council didn't accept Cesare's offer, as he probably knew they wouldn't, but it gave Cesare a chance to weigh them both. He loved the boy as did the Faenzans, and he was known to bed lads that caught his fancy, a bent that amused his men, many of whom shared the same drift.

Cesare had far bigger fish in mind than tiny Faenza but he couldn't just bypass it. It was at the entrance to the Apennines and it controlled an important route, the Via Emilia. Anyway, if he let a little fish get away, just because he liked the ruling prince, what chance would he have with bigger states? So he attacked. To his immense surprise the Faenzans defended themselves tooth and nail, even the women took up arms. Priests melted down sacred objects to provide money. The wealthy gave up their stocks of wheat and wine. The siege went on and on until the coming of winter, the winter of 1500, more than normally cold and snowy. Leaving enough men to make certain that Faenza wasn't supplied in food and weapons, Cesare went to spend winter in Cesena, a locality he liked so much he was thinking of making it, when all power was in his hands, the capital of the Romagna. He spent money like water, offering games, tournaments and processions, and organized huge festivities at Christmas and during Carnival. He showed his prowess by challenging the local boys to wrestling matches and horse races, all of which made him immensely popular. His admiration for the people of Faenza was such that when a merchant escaped Faenza and came to Cesena with important information concerning which parts of the walls were the less secure, Cesare had the man hanged.

With the coming of spring, in March to be exact, Cesare returned to Faenza where he bombarded the walls of the city for five months, concentrating on the spot revealed by the Faenzan traitor. As food and water were lacking and the dead were piling up, as there were fewer stones and hot pitch to cast down on the invaders, Astorre and the Council were obliged to seek a truce. Cesare had no reason to give the Faenzans anything. Victory was his. But he did like the lad, and it had always been his policy to be as lenient as possible with a population. In that way he could count on the defeated to provide him with food once they had returned to the fields, as well as to give shelter for his men and horses and furnish the cannon fodder--their sons--necessary to win battles. In addition, the Council paid him personally 40,000 ducats. So, good-humoredly, he offered the boy what he wanted, and the boy wanted everything. He wanted Faenza free of foreign troops, he wanted Faenzans to be able to keep their possessions, and he wanted Cesare to forbid sacking and rape. All Astorre had to do in exchange was sign over the town to Alexander VI, which he and the Council agreed to do.

Astorre and his fifteen-year-old brother Gianevangelista were given their freedom, but to Cesare's astonishment they wanted to accompany him to Rome, as today kids want to see the lights of New York. Both boys also deeply admired the most virile, courageous and experienced warrior in recent Italian history. To learn from him would make them men on the way up; Cesare was their elevator to the very top floor. It was a fatal mistake because bright lights rarely come without the accompanying greed, vice and corruption that carpet the walls in shadows.

The year was 1501. Caterina was taken to the Castel Sant'Angelo. She was said to have deeply regretted those she had murdered after the assassinations of Girolamo and Feo, a score for the first, two score for the second. Life supposedly meant little at the time, yet I remain convinced that individuals during the Renaissance wanted to live out their lives, just as we do today, to the last moment. They certainly were barbarous, hanging people until they were nearly dead and then cutting them down, still alive, so they could watch themselves be disemboweled or have their hearts cut out still beating, or, the horror of horrors, have their privates cut away and stuffed in their mouths to suffocate on. The rape of women was an essential perk of war, as was ransacking and destruction. Children died unnecessarily, some before the eyes of their parents. So Caterina had reason to repent and beg for God's forgiveness. We certainly have reason to be thankful for our own more civilized times ... if, naturally, one excludes the Great War responsible for 20,000,000 deaths, the Second that inflicted twice that, the gas chambers and, more recently, the slaughter of 8,000 boys age 13 and over in Srebrenica, all of whom certainly begged for their precious lives right up to the last horrifying second.

Caterina was taken to Castel Sant'Angelo and locked away out of the reach of those like Cesare and his close friends who would be able to crow over having possessed the charms of the Cleopatra who hadn't gotten away. Her pain deepened when she discovered that her sons, Ottaviano and Cesare, were doing just fine under the rule of Alexander, from whom both boys sought the red hat of a cardinal. With mistresses and bastards galore, they were certainly on the right path to seeing their wishes fulfilled. News from Florence informed her that her last husband's brother was dilapidating the fortune Giovanni de' Medici had willed to her and his son, little Giovanni.

At age ten Caterina had visited Florence with her father Galeazzo Marie Sforza and had been welcomed by Lorenze *Il Magnifico* himself. And now, thanks to the intervention of Louis XII, who respected her as a ruler and as a warrior, she was freed from Castel Sant'Angelo--after signing over Forlì and Imola to Alexander. As she left the castel she crossed paths with Astorre Mandredi who was being imprisoned. She made her way back to Florence, the most beautiful and cultivated city of the Renaissance, where she would die. In an ending that was almost a fairytale of beauty, she was met there by her sons Ottaviano, Cesare, Galeazzo, Sforzino, and Carlo-- the son of Feo. Her only daughter, the loyal Bianca, was also waiting for her, holding in her arms little Giovanni, the son of her last love, Giovanni, whose fortune his brother had not entirely dilapidated--in fact, there remained enough so that Caterina could live in comfort and offer sums to her sons who never ever stopped making requests for this and that, just as they had, when infants, lustily and eagerly suckled at the breasts of their wet nurses.

To save her soul she made donations to convents and churches, especially to the convent of Muratte where she asked to be interred. These donations were to Christ, for it is to Christ that women turn when they are no longer of an age to welcome virile lovers. She passed away at age forty-six. The year was 1509. Her tomb was desecrated 300 years later and her remains lost; Muratte became a prison.

But before we finish with Caterine, perhaps just a word about her last son, little Giovanni, son of Giovanni de' Medici. Different from the other Medici, he spurned intellectual activities in favor of martial interests. He often ran away from home and liked the company of simple farm boys. At age twelve he killed a boy and at age thirteen he raped a boy of sixteen. Trying desperately to save him, Florentine nobles put him under the control of an ambassador, Salviati, who was named to Rome. There Giovanni slummed with lowlifes, in perpetual trouble. He became a condottiere and was known for exclaiming, "I rule with my ass in the saddle and a sword in my fist!" Pope Leo X chose him first to police Rome and then to form an army using men of normally irredeemable depravity that only he had the force to make into manageable soldiers. He specialized in lightning strikes with a preference for ambushes. His motto was, "I embrace my rivals in order to strangle them." When his patron Pope Leo X died, Giovanni added black stripes to his armor, for which he is known historically as Giovanni dalle Bande Nere. He married Salviati's daughter and had a son destined to become lord of Florence. Severely wounded in battle, he had to have his foot amputated; ten men were needed to hold him down. He died five days later of gangrene. He was the very last of the condottieri. Of his direct descendants, other than fathering a Florentine lord, one, Marie de' Medici, became Queen of France--but led a terribly sorrowful life. (The Florentine lord he sired was Cosimo I who would rule Florence, employ Michelangelo, and encourage Cellini to give birth to a miracle equal to Michelangelo's *David*, Cellini's *Perseus*.)

For Cesare, Forlì and Imola were an interlude to much bigger acts of bravura. He went on to take Urbino, the citadel of the Montefeltro, and a dozen other city-states. Along the way he heard stories about some of his captains, traitors in the pay of Roman nobles eager for the reign of Alexander to come to an end by assassinating their leader, Cesare. He invited them to a dinner at one of his palaces and on an agreed signal troops surrounded and dispatched them all. He moved on to Siena, sacking, destroying, maiming, killing and raping. Those who wouldn't give up their money were tortured; if they were found to have nothing to give up, their throats were slashed (the soldiers were instructed that this was the best way to kill without blunting a sharp sword or dagger against bone).

Cesare was no fool. He knew his father would not live on forever. He had thusly looted Italy of every ducat available, he had storerooms of weapons at his disposal and his troops loved this handsome fearless man who conceded their every wish as long as they remained loyal to him. What he didn't count on was *his* nearly dying at exactly the same time as his father, which is precisely what happened. What he didn't count on either was the election of a new pope as vigorous, intelligent and belligerent as Alexander had been.

He and his father had been invited to a banquet after which they both fell seriously ill. Illness was nothing new to the Renaissance. I haven't gone into the subject, but all the actors in this book, all without exception, had fallen ill multiple times throughout their lives. Lucrezia, for example, could nearly be described as being continuously sick--especially following her many miscarriages. Illness came from literally everywhere, bad food, incredibly diseased water that one drank or swam in; illness came from common flue, from typhus, cholera and malaria; from flees and rats and dogs and other people. Illness came through breathing, sweating, defecating and fucking. Illness favored the months of July and August, hot muggy months propitious to dysentery. All of Alexander's predecessors, Innocent, Sixtus, Pius and Calixtus had died during those months. And it was now July and both Cesare and Alexander were at death's door. Perhaps they believed, as did the people, that they had been poisoned during the banquet. Perhaps, as some said, they themselves had tried to poison their host--an ever-criticizing cardinal they both could well do without--but somehow they had drunk their own means of murder. As Alexander was now seventy-three, he was in more danger than his young son. They were both bled although, unlike his father, Cesare was plunged into cold water, the accepted cure for fever. Alexander received last rites but not Cesare, a former cardinal, who vaunted his atheism.

Alexander died and nearly overnight Cesare lost it all. His palaces were sacked and the lands he had conquered were recovered by the counts, lords, dukes and princes he had overturned. He was carried away by litter to recuperate at his sister's retreat of Nepi. In Rome Pius III was elected but immediately passed away, replaced by the powerful Julius II, a mortal enemy of the Borgia. The conclave, which had felt itself so threatened that it met in the Castel Sant'Angelo, had lasted a single day, one of the shortest in history. Strong in body and mind, intelligent, handsome, arrogant and utterly ruthless, the new pope had contracted syphilis but with age he replaced the lust of the loins with that of the stomach, devoting himself to roast pig and strong wines. His temperament was described as melancholic, capable of the greatest furies. He created the Swiss Guard and put Michelangelo to work on the Sistine Chapel (and the Guard's uniforms). He refused Henry VIII's divorce, ending the Catholic Church in England, and he brought war and peace to the continent according to his whims, and was only prevented from uniting Italy into one country by the emergence of someone still more powerful than he, the Grim Reaper.

Julius issued a warrant for the arrest of Cesare, accusing him of the murders of his brother Juan, his sister's husband Alfonso, Astorre Manfredi and Astorre's brother, as well as many others. But in exchange for his giving up the wealth he had hoarded and the fortifications in the Romagna still in possession of those who remained loyal to him, Cesare was allowed exile in Spain. He retired to Chinchilla, a mountain castle in the heights near Valencia.

Cesare's rout was such that even King Louis XII, who had called him his dear son, sent word to Ferrara and Alfonso, Lucrezia's husband, that he was free to leave her as France no longer recognized her as being his legitimate wife. Luckily for Lucrezia, Alfonso had grown to love her, and this despite the fact that she had never stopped welcoming lovers into her bed. Other scandals continued to haunt her. One of Alfonso's brothers, Ippolito, who happened to also be a cardinal and was known for his unbounded lustfulness, had fallen in love with a local beauty. The girl claimed that she far preferred another of Ippolito's brothers, Giulio, whose beautiful brown eyes alone were worth more than all of Ippolito. In response the cardinal waylaid his brother and tried to cut out those wonderful eyes. Alfonso forced Ippolito to ask for pardon, but as Giulio suffered horrible pain and the near total loss of sight, he decided to get revenge on both brothers, Alfonso and Ippolito, by having them killed. He united his forces with still another of his brothers, Ferrante. Their conspiracy was discovered, however, and although Alfonso would not have them executed, he did send them to prison. Ferrante died in his dungeon forty-three years later, Giulio endured for fifty-three.

Caterina gave herself to Christ; Lucrezia, despite ever-increasing amounts of donations to convents and churches as she grew older, never abandoned that part of herself that wanted to be a woman to men of flesh and blood. Right up to the end she continued affairs with men, the two most important being Francesco Gonzaga and Pietro Bembo, for whom she wrote letters of stupefying sensuality (for the period).

Right up to the finish line she continued to give Alfonso children, five in all. At age thirty-nine she died giving birth, birth to a child and birth to a star, her star, that shines as brightly now as it did 500 years ago, solid proof that it is better to use life and be used by it than to flee the storm, dodging the droplets, seeking an illusive shelter that exists, in the end, for none of us.

In the mountain retreat of Chinchilla things went wrong for Cesare when his exile turned into captivity. Isabella of Spain decided to follow Julius' lead in prosecuting him for the deaths of his brother Juan, duke of Gadía, and Lucrezia's husband, Alfonso of Aragon, both of Spanish lineage. He escaped, climbing down a rope. He made his way by boat and trek to Pamplona in Navarre, to his brother-in-law Juan of Navarre who put him at the head of his troops. As the city-states in Spain were in constant upheaval just like their Italian counterparts, Cesare was constantly at war. His last day found him chasing a band of rebels. At age thirty-one he was still in the full glory of his bravado and virility and so thought nothing of outdistancing his men. Alas, the rebels he was chasing turned to face him and, highly outnumbered, he received many blows, one of which was the fatal plunge of a dagger to his throat, just above the armor. He fell into a ravine, just like Catherine's stable boy husband, Feo; he was stripped naked as Feo had been; but his genitals had not been mutilated, as Feo's--his were covered by a rock by one of the attackers who recognized him. Juan of Navarre had the body buried in the small church of Viana where it lies to this day. Cesare often compared himself to that other Caesar, and as they died just hours apart it can perhaps be said for one as for the other: *Aut Caesar, aut nihil*! -- Either Caesar, or nothing! The year was 1507.

In the spring of 1501 a new prisoner was added to Castel Sant'Angelo on the very day that Caterina was freed. Astorre Manfredi, her would-be son-in-law, had lost the town of Faenza to Cesare after a brave defense. He and his brother Gianevangelista had accompanied Cesare to Rome to learn about life and war. But unlike Caterina, the young nobleman had not earned the admiration of the French and was consigned to the lowest cells. In 1502 the unfortunate boy suffered the fate that Caterina escaped: he was strangled in the prison and his body dumped into the Tiber. Johann Burchard wrote that both boys had been participants in an orgy along with a large number of very young girls. Whether they freely consented to take part or were forced to will never be known. Whether the orgy even took place will never be known. Cesare was said to have been involved--it would have been far from his first. Perhaps his father took part too. Burchard only says that "a certain powerful person sated his lust" on the boy. Machiavelli gets into the act too because he was there, physically there to give Cesare advice, one piece of which we find in his book: "When a prince assumes power over a conquered territory his first obligation, if he wishes to preserve that power, is to destroy the rulers in place." Every time, in Italian politics, that this principle hadn't been observed, the prince lived to regret it. It's true that had the boy lived he might have eventually become a problem for Cesare. Already immensely popular in his hometown, Astorre might have outshone Cesare himself in public adulation, an intolerable risk to a man who wore impeccable black velvet and paraded around on a white charger adorned with bells, his stirrups made of gold, but a man who was aging, a man with "flowers".

Burchard says that Astorre and his brother Gianevangelista were fished from the Tiber, attached together with a stone tied to their necks. The bodies of the aforementioned females were also discovered, tied together in the same fashion. The boys' bodies had torture marks. Cesare pushed his fiendishness to extremes by greeting an envoy from Venice and springing on him the news of the murders, knowing that Venice had taken a special and highly favorable interest in both Faenza and Astorre Manfredi. The envoy was said to have not even blinked, unsurprising for a city where slaves could still be purchased, their prices varying from six ducats for a man to a hundred for a beddable girl. Burchard ends his story of Astorre by saying that "The young man was of such unequaled beauty and intelligence that it would be impossible to find another as sterling as he in all of Italy.''

The boy was 17.

The year was 1502.

This long incursion into Italian history is the décor into which Caravaggio was born.

Interlude

The Lute Player

The Lute Player exists in three versions. Vasari, the extremely important author of *Lives of the Most Excellent Painters, Sculptors and Architects,* noted the exquisite detail found on the carafe of water, reflecting the window and room, a carafe filled with flowers on which one sees even the dew. The model is unknown but may have been Mario Minniti, although in other pictures Minniti comes through far more masculine than in *The Lute Player*. This is why it's generally believed that the boy was the castrato Pedro Montoya who lived in the Palazzo Madama. Castrati were extremely prized at the time for their voices and feminine looks (for those who have a taste for androgynous lads).

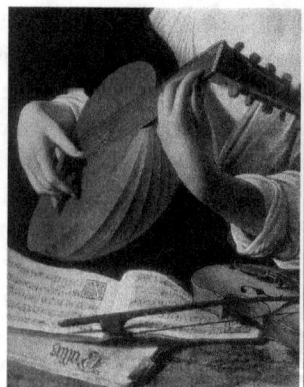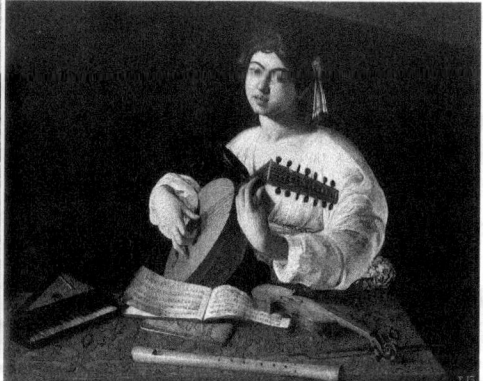

The Lute Player

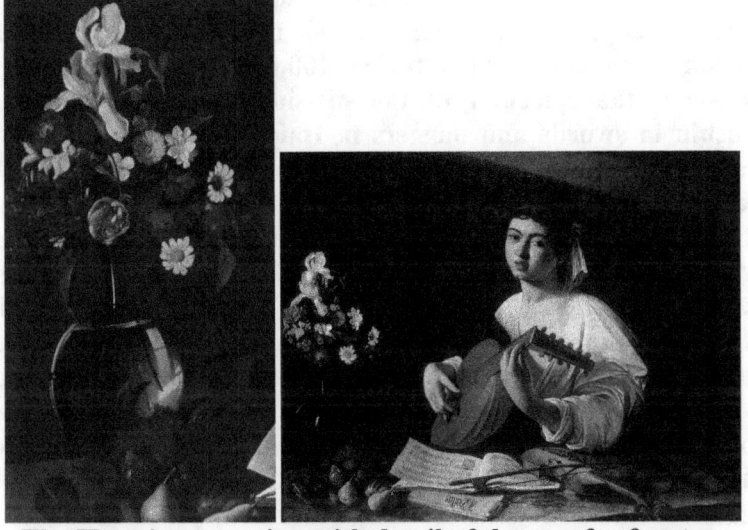

The Hermitage version with detail of the carafe of water.

CHAPTER THREE

- 1 -

Michelangelo Merisi da Caravaggio was born around 1571. Famous while he lived, he was immediately forgotten after his death, to be rediscovered in the twentieth century. He was blessed with two beautiful names, *Michelangelo* which evoked the famous Florentine genius, although Caravaggio's first name had been chosen after the feast day on which he had been born, Archangel Michael, and *Caravaggio*, the site of his birth. His father, Fermo Merisi, was the chief architect of the Colonna family household, a family known for its military glory, and he directed its staff. Some say Fermo was a mason, which may have been the case before the Colonna opened wider horizons. He was responsible for the palace servants, cooks, valets, coachmen, among others. One person especially stands out during Caravaggio's youth, Constanza Colonna, who took an interest in the son of her servant. We'll meet her later when she comes to the rescue of Caravaggio, but for the moment she weds, at age 12, Francesco Sforza, 17, a marriage that starts off so poorly that she threatens to kill herself if her father doesn't free her: ''If you don't get me out of his house I'll kill myself and my lost soul be damned!'' As the Colonna carried weight, the pope allowed her to enter a nunnery where she gave birth to a son, signifying the consummation of the marriage. Five other sons followed, a certain sign that she had somehow found her husband less boorish than at first. Two of her boys would turn out to be as uncontrollable as Caravaggio, but without his artistic gifts, all would be valiant warriors.

A two-hour ride from the stiflingly dead town of Caravaggio brought one to the big city, Milan, under Spanish rule at the time, the bustling center of commerce and manufacturing, 100,000 souls--as many as London and Paris--and the epicenter of the silk industry as well as the finest workmanship in swords and daggers in Italy. Gold from the New World caused a rise in prices in Milan that impoverished the majority of the Milanese, and what had been considered a miracle of riches would soon lead to the bankruptcy of Spain. Milan was inhabited by the young Caravaggio until he went to Florence, later in our story, at the age of 21. Florence was the capital of art, and da Vinci and Michelangelo, soon followed by Raphael, were its kings. What a change Caravaggio would bring to all this. Already Michelangelo was known for his nudes, the genitals of which would be later painted over. But how different were his naked boys from Caravaggio's. Michelangelo's muscular lads looked as fresh and scrubbed as if they'd just stepped out of an hour-long shower. Caravaggio's were so realistic that one could nearly whiff the pheromones from the lads' beautiful but slightly rank bodies, and in his *Jupiter, Neptune and Pluto* we have a full under view of Neptune's pubic bush, scrotum and penis with its full prepuce. And even when just sitting, surrounded by fruit or flowers, the shirts are suggestively open over their naked chests, often shiny with sweat as if they've just left a bed after making sweet love, the eyes languorous.

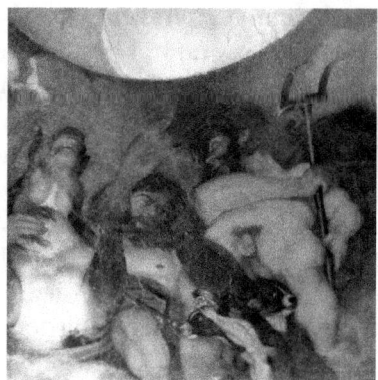

Jupiter, Neptune and Pluto

In the book *Who's Who in Gay and Lesbian History* the writer says that Caravaggio's *Amore vincitore* makes him think of a "completely naked pin-up teenager," which underlines the sexiness of his paintings, even though, in the case of the *Amore vincitore*, it's not the naked pin-up of a teenager I'd have in *my* bedroom. *Love conquers all; let us all live for love* is Caravaggio's illustration of Virgil's lines, a painting universally adored, the perfect depiction of the guileless innocence of boys. Everything about the lad brings joy to the heart, this painting of Cecco. Cecco was Caravaggio's lover, even if there was a misconception that seemed to affirm their liaison: an artist had written in a letter to a friend, "the painting shows Cecco who lays with Caravaggio." Supposedly, *lay*, in the English of that time, meant "to live with." Supposedly.

Painted for Vincenzo Giustiniani, it was the crown jewel of his collection. Giustiniani was a very important art collector, especially of the works of Caravaggio, whose assembled paintings are found in the Palazzo Giustiniani near the Pantheon in Rome, 300 paintings, 15 by Caravaggio, and 1,200 sculptures. A banker and one of the richest men in Italy, he was aided in his collection by his cardinal brother Benedetto.

Still again we have Caravaggio's realism. The dirt under the finger and toenails, the crooked teeth and heart-rending laugh, the lad thrilled to be dressing as for carnival in angel wings, with the bow and arrows every boy loves to wield. There was no question of immodesty, as at the time lads plunged naked into the Arno and Tiber.

That said, most reviewers nonetheless note the bared shoulders, the enticing smile, sensuous lips, exposed genitals and cleavage of the boy's buttocks.

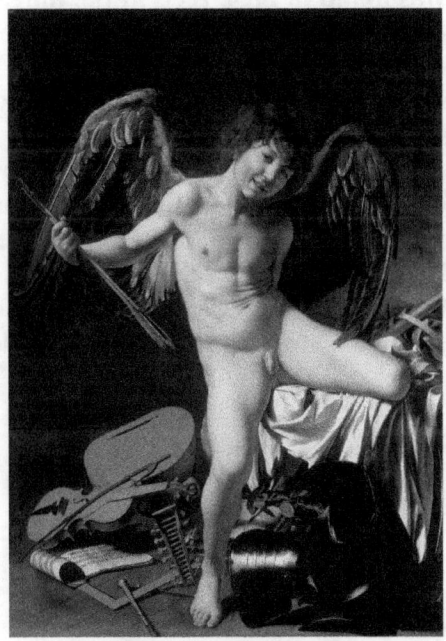

Amor Vincit Omnia

As far as realism goes, nothing is more ghastly than the blood spurting from the jugular vein of a tyrant, sectioned by a sword in his *Judith Beheading Holofernes*. The realism in his paintings was such that he even showed the dirt under the toenails!

In the painting *Judith Beheading Holofernes* Judith saves Israel by seducing the Assyrian general Holofernes, getting him drunk enough so that she could slip away from his nude body, on its back, and slice through the carotid, severing the head with the general's own sword he had left hanging above his bed. X-rays show that she had left the bed raped and naked, although in other interpretations she may have done no more than show him her breasts to spur him on, the nipples of which, in the painting, are erotically erect. The payment for whatever she did was his head exposed on a lance from the walls of Bethulia, thereby scaring the Assyrians into panicked retreat. The painting shows the exact moment of Holofernes' passing from life to death, the eyes wild with fear, the body arched in an orgasmic spasm, ropes of blood spurting into the pillows.

Some believe that the accuracy of the beheading is due to Caravaggio's having witnessed the crime of the century, the Cenci murder and beheading in 1599, fully covered elsewhere in this book.

Judith was modeled by a Caravaggio whore, Fillide Melandroni, one he used in several paintings, an extremely beautiful and pure-looking specimen of what was found in the streets at the time, a perfect Madonna or Magdalene. In the painting Judith demonstrates incredible determination and disgust, total hatred for Holofernes' rape of both Israel and her body.

The details in Caravaggio's *oeuvre* are overpowering: dirt under the fingernails, feet soiled, teeth stained; the servant Abra's sun-wrinkled leathery skin and the grey hair peeking from under her cap, holding the bag that will receive the head; Holofernes' muscles and horrified expression; Judith's knitted brow; and the blood, spurting onto the sweat-soaked bed while Holofernes clutches the white sheets.

Painted at the very end of the 1500s, the painting was lost until rediscovered in 1950. It is considered his first violent painting, opening what became floodgates of hypnotizing horror.

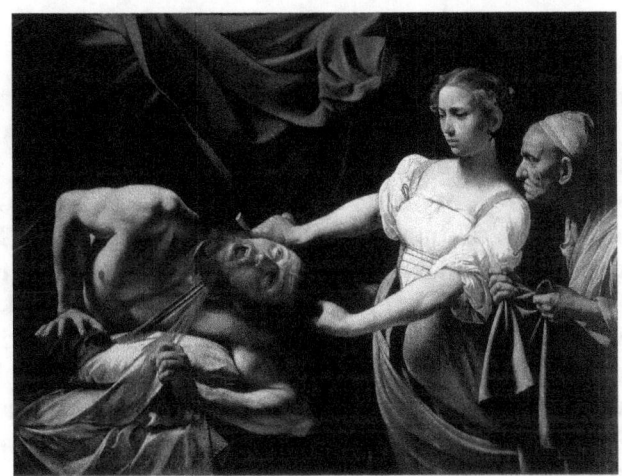

Judith Beheading Holofernes

- 2 -

But all this is in the future. For the moment he's 13 and apprenticed to Simone Peterzano, a painter of mediocre repute who taught the boy little except for a smidgen of drawing, stretching canvases and the art of grounding colors. Caravaggio is thought to have been rowdy even at that age, controlled with difficulty. He ran around with gangs as he did later in life, and he certainly had his first sexual experiences with boys and whores. And as Milan was noted for its violence he may have done more, he may have killed someone, as is suggested in several texts, but at any rate he left the city, never to return, and headed south to his destiny in Rome.

The city he entered, Rome, where he would spend the next 14 years, had once been like Caravaggio in a new array of the best clothes, it had been the center of the ancient world and had reigned supreme for half a millennium, but now it was decrepit, the buildings crumpling among fields of mud, rats and stench, with only a few favored islets inhabited by the rich and powerful. During the emperors there had been 1,000,000 souls, now there were 100,000. Then as today the Romans rose early, slept the sweltering afternoons away and spent the nights in earthly amusement. The city was violent, the streets unsafe, men carried stilettos and swords, and the most vile could poison an enemy through the prick of a death ring.

He was described as being handsome in a wild way; his hair, curly and unruly, his eyes large and wide like a Spaniards, his clothes said to have been of the best quality and cut, but worn until they were nearly rags.

Caravaggio spent much time with his friends roaming the vicinity of the Piazza Navona and, if they wanted sex, the Piazza del Popolo where women and boys plied their trade in ill-lit alleys or behind the parted curtains from their lodgings where they appeared naked, enticing men who often found that what they were buying was far more sordid than what they could get for free among their own sex.

The pope at the time was Clement VIII, intelligent, prudent, ruthless and having an excellent head for business. He allowed Jews to live in only Ancona, Rome and Avignon, and forbade them from selling "new" products, putting them at an economic disadvantage. He burned Giordano Bruno at the stake: a mathematician, philosopher and poet, Bruno believed the earth turned around the sun and was, although a friar, an atheist. Clement initiated excellent relations with Henry IV, thanks to which, in part, Henry converted to Catholicism, Clement's greatest triumph (10). He tried the same coup with the Protestant James I of England but failed (11). Another huge accomplishment was adding Ferrara to the Papal States when the Este no longer produced male heirs. He also banned weapons in Rome and outlawed dueling, both of which would cause Caravaggio and others to lie following the killing of Tomassoni. Clement was determined to make Rome the center of art in Italy, to the benefit of Caravaggio and countless other painters, sculptors and architects.

It is said that Caravaggio, Reni and Ribera were highly influenced by the Council of Trent and its attempt at a counter-reformation that would end the sale of indulgences, impose religious subjects in art, outlaw nudity and reduce church music to Gregorian chants. Even before the council Pope Adrian VI envisioned painting over the scandalous nakedness of Michelangelo's works in the Sistine Chapel, a plan happily ending with the pope's demise. Caravaggio himself was supposed to have been influenced by the Milanese cardinal Borromeo, a sincere ascetic who slept on straw, sold his furniture to provide money for the poor and organized succor for the sick and needy during the terrible Milanese plague of 1576-1578 which claimed 25,000. When dead, Borromeo was embalmed and put on display for the weeping and howling multitudes that passed before his body, touching his feet with crosses and rosaries. A bare 26 years later the desiccated blackened remains, smothered in gifts of diamonds, emeralds, rubies and sapphires, were canonized.

The church held forth against the superfluous, the elegant, the pagan and the naked, yet what followed was the ridiculous bling-bling of the baroque and the eroticism of nude Sebastians (12), infinitely more sexually stirring than anything envisioned by Michelangelo, other than his *David*, and John the Baptist's head severed in painting after painting, blood gushing, eyes gaping, teeth bared, tongues engorged, and mouths frozen in silent screams, were infinitely more realistic after the Counter-Reformation. On the sexual front, no artist, with the possible exception of Reni, refused himself access to an apprentice's or a model's muscular buttocks. (Reni was either too discreet to be found out or so pure that many maintained he died a virgin [1].)

Caravaggio was eternally dissatisfied. We don't know why, although having lost most of his family to the plague so young may have been a factor. Cellini was eternally hot-headed, another of Caravaggio's characteristics, even though no boy had been more desired by his father than Cellini, and no boy more worshipped after his birth than Cellini by his dad. Cellini was nonetheless touchy and turned to vengeful murder on more than one occasion, as did Caravaggio. Both Cellini and Caravaggio were alike too in being intrepid workers. In Caravaggio's case he turned out painting after painting, and the more depressed he was--the more the Fates seemed to malign him--the more he churned out masterpieces. Both Cellini and Caravaggio also preferred boys, Caravaggio Minniti and Cecco, Cellini too many to list (6). Caravaggio was an earthy realist. His paintings show dirty feet, soiled hands and filthy fingernails, rigorous right down to their grooves. Caravaggio makes one think of an animal, with an animal's spontaneity and boldness; there was nothing shy or hesitant about him. If he had to kiss his masters' feet and hands it was with the awareness that he could just as easily bite and, if need be, go for the jugular with the dagger he was never without. Reality in painting, reality in life: this was Caravaggio's creed. He rejected the silly artifice of both mannerism and the baroque. He lived in the post-Reformation world but was untouched by the jeweled, perfumed hands that signed the decrees issued by the Council of Trent. And he would eventually die in the same way, on a deserted beach, in a humble hut among strangers, a man possessed by his art until his dying breath, a man as humble as those who would bury him, as fiercely arrogant as are those deprived of the world's greatest treasure: its love.

Few paintings represent Caravaggio realism as does *The Incredulity of Saint Thomas*:

The Incredulity of Saint Thomas was painted c.1601-1602 and is now found in the Sanssouci Picture Gallery in Potsdam Germany. In the age in which we live today, that of realism, there are few better representatives than this painting by Caravaggio. In John 20:25 Thomas states, ''Unless I see the nail marks in his hands and put my fingers where the nails were, and put my hand into his side, I will not believe it.'' The painting is a chief example of chiaroscuro, the contrast in light and dark so great that the painting appears three-dimensional. The miracle of Christ's resurrection is seconded by the miracle of the painting having survived the bombings of W.W. II. A second version of the painting has recently come to light in Trieste, and authenticated by numerous experts.

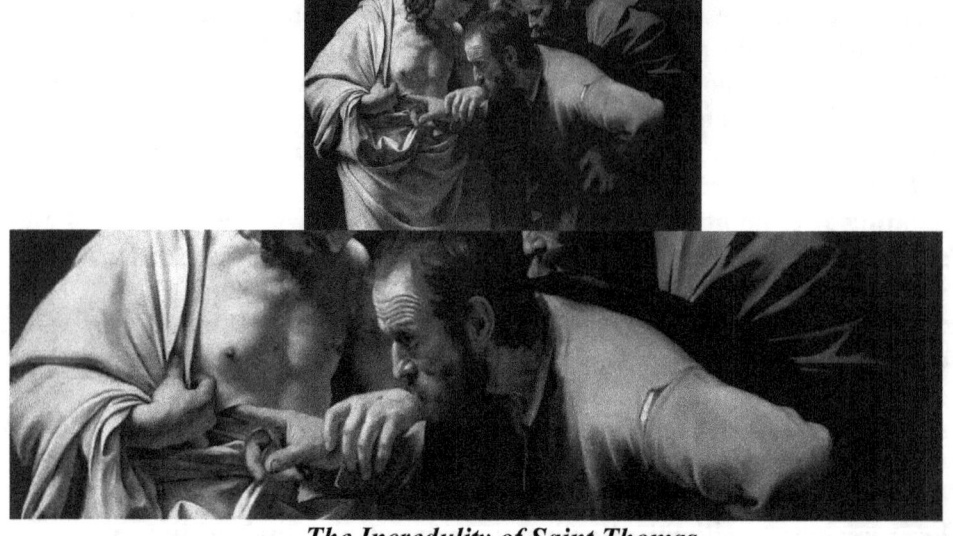

The Incredulity of Saint Thomas

- 3 -

Popes and cardinals like del Monte owed their enormous influence to popes such as Alexander VI whom we've met, and thanks, too, to an even more powerful pope, so powerful intellectually and so powerful militarily that he has come down to us as the Warrior Pope: Jules II.

Julius II was different from the other popes, with the exception of Alexander, in having balls, big brass balls not unlike those shown peeking through the waist-length armor of Leonidas, whose statue, on a high pedestal, is in the midst of the Greek town of Sparta, should you ever get that way.

Lodovico Guicciardini, the great Florentine historian, alive at the time, had this to say about Julius: "He was a soldier in a cassock; he drank and swore heavily as he led his troops; he was willful, coarse, bad-tempered and difficult to manage. He would ride his horse up the Lateran stairs to his papal bedroom and tether it at the door." And he loved being called the Warrior Pope.

Peter O'Toole portrayed him perfectly in the series *The Tudors*, both his character and physically, but only at the very end of his life did he resemble the painting by Raphael where he comes through weak and sickly, inappropriate for a man who had led armies and reigned supreme over European diplomacy. Raphael shows him wearing a beard, a practice forbidden by canon law, but Julius only did so for a year as a sign of mourning at the loss of Bologna, a vital Papal State.

Born Giuliano della Rovere (we'll call him della Rovere until he becomes pope), he may have been both the son *and* lover of Sixtus IV, an accusation made also against Alexander VI and *his* bastard son Cesare (several sources, existent at the time, maintain that this was so, but then Julius and Sixtus, Alexander and Cesare, had many enemies). He was educated among Franciscans by Sixtus himself, and was Sixtus' altar boy when Sixtus became pope. Sixtus endowed della Rovere with numerous bishoprics, making him a wealthy young man. He was a papal legate in France for four years, which served him mightily when Alexander became pope and Julius had to flee to France to escape Alexander's wrath because Julius had accused him of buying the papal election. He convinced the French king Charles VIII to intervene in Italian affairs by invading Italy, but Alexander, subtle, intelligent and *in power*, outmatched della Rovere who had to wait for Alexander's death to have a try at the Vatican, but another was elected, Pope Pius III, who luckily had only 26 days to live. In the meantime della Rovere gained Cesare's support due to Cesare's illness which nearly finished him off, and due to della Rovere's promise to reinstate Cesare as head of papal troops and assure him that he would retain all of the land he had conquered under his father Alexander. Cesare was no fool except this one time. He gave his support to della Rovere who was unanimously elected pope except for two votes, della Rovere's own and the French Cardinal d'Amboise who wanted the job for the glory of France (receiving della Rovere's vote, out of friendship, in the attempt). Naturally, the usual bribes--money and a mightier position in the food chain--won the day. Cesare was killed, as related earlier, and Julius II erased every remaining trace of Alexander. Nigel Cawthorne quoted Julius as saying, ''I will not live in the same rooms as the Borgias. Alexander desecrated the Holy Church as none before. He usurped the papal power by the devil's aid, and I forbid under the pain of excommunication anyone to speak or think of Borgia again. His name and memory must be forgotten. It must be crossed out of every document and memorial. His reign must be obliterated. All paintings made of the Borgias or for them must be covered over with black crepe. All the tombs of the Borgias must be opened and their bodies sent back to where they belong--to Spain.'' The Borgia apartments would remain sealed for over 300 years!

One of the major problems for the new pope was Henry VIII who wanted a divorce. A papal dispensation had already allowed Henry to marry Catherine of Aragon who had been Henry's brother's bride for six months before he died, leaving Catherine a virgin as he had been too ill to be operative--although the day after the wedding he bragged to his friends, ''Last night I visited the depths of Spain.'' The refusal to allow the divorce would end Catholicism in England, all because the king wanted to fuck his way through five additional wives.

The second problem was the Papal States, governed by lords, dukes, and princes that the pope wanted returned to the bosom of the church, after which he was determined to unite all of Italy. But he died too soon, of fever, to accomplish this last dream.

He had put Michelangelo to the task of constructing his tomb, commissioned in 1505 and finished in 1545. It was originally intended for St. Peter's Basilica but wound up in the church of San Pietro in Vincoli. Although the actual tomb is colossal, with 7 statues, including the magnificent Moses, the original would have been far bigger, comprising 40 statues, some of the unfinished ones now on view in the Louvre. Only the Moses has a commanding presence and an anecdote has it that it was so lifelike that when finished Michelangelo struck it on the knee with a hammer, saying "NOW SPEAK!" The hammer mark can be seen today. As for Julius, he was buried far from his monument, in St. Peter's Basilica.

Michelangelo had also been appointed to paint the Sistine Chapel, named after Sixtus IV who restored it. Julius was said to have appreciated the physical beauties of the men painted by Michelangelo but part of their beauty was destroyed forever when one of Michelangelo's associates, Daniele da Volterra, was ordered to cover up the genitals following the genius's death. But he didn't touch the acorns and oak leaves present, the first representing the male glans and the second the renewal of sexuality, among other things. The central *Creation of Adam* is certainly the most stirring work of art known to humanity.

One of Julius' lovers is thought to have been Giovanni Alidosi who accompanied della Rovere to France. Julius made him a cardinal and he served as an intermediary between the pope and Michelangelo, as both were headstrong and difficult (just the negotiations concerning the Sistine Chapel, before a single brush stroke, took two years). As mentioned above, Julius lost Bologna and as a consequence Alidosi had three persons found guilty of aiding both the Bolognese and the Venetians. They were strangled to death under his orders. Of Alidosi, cardinal Bembo said, "Faith meant nothing to him, nor religion, nor trustworthiness, nor shame, nor anything that was holy." Much hated, Alidosi was often caught and tried by various rulers, notably those of Bologna and Urbino, ruled by the pope's nephew, Francesco Maria della Rovere, but instead of dispatching the reviled cardinal he was always given a trial, time enough for Julius to intervene in his favor. As Francesco had been appointed general to conquer Bologna and had failed to do so, he was summoned to Rome to explain himself to his uncle the pope. After the meeting, while heading back to his lodgings on horseback, accompanied by a group of his soldiers, he crossed the path of Alidosi who was on his way to dine with the pope. Alidosi saluted Francesco in an arrogant way that displeased one of Francesco's followers, just a youngster, who dismounted and knifed Alidosi, sitting on his mule, in the throat. From then on it was an eating-frenzy of boys out to kill each other. Francesco's men won out, and while Alidosi's men went scurrying away, Francesco's took turns slicing off pieces of Alidosi's face and plunging daggers into his body. Julius had the pieces interred and realpolitik obliging, suffered his pain in private.

Another lover was supposedly Luigi Pulci, a poet described by Cellini as being beautiful and talented. The Venetian diarist Girolamo Priuli maintains that Julius brought to Rome "some very handsome young men with whom he was publicly rumored to have sex, and he was said to be the passive partner." When attacking Bologna a sonnet circulated, advising Julius to return to Rome where he could content himself with "Squarcia and Curzio in your holy palace/keeping the bottle in your mouth and a cock up your ass." It *was* true that he drank a lot.

Julius made plans to demolish the old basilica of St. Peter's and replace it with a huge basilica, the whole serving to house Julius' final resting place, the greatest tomb ever erected. Michelangelo was chosen to design it as well as to build the basilica, but over the next 120 years the combined efforts of popes and architects were needed to see it through. It is believed that St. Peter was crucified there, at the emplacement of the current obelisk, by Nero who held the Christians responsible for the burning of the city. As for Julius, Michelangelo finally finished his tomb after 40 years of bargaining and labor. Julius wasn't interred there though. For all his efforts he was accorded a simple slab of marble on the floor of the basilica, that people walk over every day, little aware of the headstrong warrior beneath.

– 4 –

Another warrior in another part of the world was amassing the wealth that filtered down through the hands of the nobility and the clergy into those of artists such as Caravaggio. Word had reached Europe of an empire of incredible cruelty and unimaginable treasures. Hernán Cortés landed off the coast of the New World in 1519 with a fleet of 11 ships, 500 men and 13 horses, plus harquebusiers, crossbows and small cannons. Commandeering sand dunes on which he and his men built shacks for shelter and shade, many immediately fell ill to the foul water which provoked diarrhea, the first, and most humiliating, cause of death among warriors. Then came oppressive heat, humidity that rusted a man's joints and brought on cramps, sand flies and clouds of mosquitoes that tortured the skin and sun that burned it. Imprisoned in their stifling armor for fear of native arrows and spears, their faces masked behind beards and their bodies stinking with sweat, this was the destiny of the conquerors until they eventually vanquished the Aztecs.

Greeted by natives, some of whom would accept them long enough to search out their week points, others who attacked immediately. The Spaniards, thanks to their firearms, armor and expertise in wielding swords, and their unequaled military discipline, shot and stabbed their way through the hundreds of naked bodies that presented themselves in wave after wave.

In his capital of Tenochtitlán, Montezuma followed the invaders' progress thanks to daily messages from his spies. Climbing to the top of his pyramid temple, dedicated to the hummingbird god of war and sacrifice Huitzilopochtli, he spent the nights in prayer, undecided as to the provenance of the invaders, whether they were the promised god Quetzalcoatl or others, while the hearts of twelve boys, freshly sacrificed, extracted from their chests while still alive, their screams as habitual as the blood caked hair of Montezuma's priests, sizzled on an adjoining brazier.

The first shock awaiting Cortés as he left the beach for the interior was the discovery of a temple where fifty boys had been fleshly sacrificed, their blood and viscera forming huge puddles, the walls of the temple blackened from the splatter, the hearts, now silent, on a nearby ledge.

In another village, one that had welcomed Cortés after learning of his mysterious weapons that expulsed lightning and thunder, Cortés came upon his first veritable Aztecs, nobility sent to collect taxes and boys for sacrifices, girls for Montezuma and his court. The Aztecs wandered past the Spaniards as if they were invisible, holding roses to their noses against the men's stench, their shoulders caped with magnificent bird feathers, sign of their nobility. Cortés had them imprisoned by the natives who had gone over to his side, happy to no longer be obliged to pay taxes and surrender their youths. Cortés told the natives that he would take the Aztecs to his ships from which they could not escape. But once they reached the beach he freed the Aztecs with presents for themselves and for Montezuma.

In another town Cortés had their temple gods--that his men shoved down the stairs of the pyramid--replaced by a cross once the floor and walls had been washed. The natives looked on in disbelief, which was nothing in comparison with their surprise to see the sun rise the next morning without the aid of human sacrifices the day before.

Once the Spanish had harvested a good amount of gold, jewels and feathered finery, the men wished to return home. With revolt in the air, Cortés had a ship loaded with every ounce of accumulated wealth, a bribe for Charles V, to win his goodwill. Then potential leaders of revolt were ferreted out and executed, and Cortés had all his ships scuttled to make retreat impossible.

Cortés made a ''blood and tears'' speech which gave courage to his soldiers, and then they entered the interior of a world that we, with all our science, scarcely comprehend to this day. How can one understand the incredible courage of these men who set off into the unknown, just as, years later, other men, of equal courage, led civilization to the moon? At the same time, how is it possible to justify the thousands who found immediate death at the end of the Spaniards' swords and, later on, the hundreds of thousands more who were disfigured and massacred by the diseases brought to these newly discovered lands by the discoverers? Cortés faced tribes of thousands, tribes he incredibly, mysteriously vanquished when one considers the handful of Spaniards on one side and the Aztecs who numbered at least a million warriors on the other. He passed near active volcanoes, so close that some of his men's shirts caught fire. They knew nights well below zero, where some froze to death in their sleep, cols deep with snow, days of feverish heat, yet they were always fully armed and armored in case of enemy attack. At one location Cortés came across a temple surrounded by thousands of human skulls and strewn with the still warm bodies of disemboweled sacrificial victims, ready to be eaten, blood and blood-stink everywhere. At another village he was welcomed by a priest who allowed him to admire their ceremony, the young boy pinned down by two men, one holding firm each arm while a third put a collar around the boy's throat to lessen his squirming. The priest held high the obsidian knife he plunged into the young heaving chest, slitting it open, extracting the warm, beating heart he held toward the sun, assurance that the sun would rise the following day. Buddy Levy, in his wonderful *Cortés*, tells us that there were other rituals involving "the slashing open of the throats of infants, the beheading of young women and the dressing of teenagers in recently flayed human skin."

At Tlaxcala his group of less than 400 men met and defeated 40,000 Tlaxcalan warriors, battle after battle as the Tlaxcalan chiefs tried every possible way that would lead to victory over the Spaniards, after which the white devil would be sacrificed and eaten. Yet not one single Spaniard was killed (the wounded were carefully hidden from Tlaxcalan eyes), and in the end the Tlaxcalans brought hundreds of turkeys and baskets of maize cakes to feed their new masters. They then put their whole army at Cortés' disposal.

When Montezuma heard about the victory he was amazed, as the Tlaxcalans were the only tribe he himself had failed to subdue.

From a distance Cortés could see Montezuma's capital, Tenochtitlán, that seemed to float in Lake Texcoco, moored in place by extremely narrow causeways made of stone and, in places, as long as five miles. The city was so magnificent Cortés named it the City of Dreams. It was perhaps also the most populated city in the world at that time. After much prayer Montezuma decided to receive Cortés. He sent an impersonator to great him, accompanied by sorcerers whose task it was to make the Spanish fall ill and die. Cortés was offered feathers and gold, the sight of which made his men so mad with gold lust that they literally drooled at the mouth, incomprehensible to the Aztecs because for them gold was of far less importance than jade and their beautiful feathers.

The city consisted of multistoried buildings and villas, terraces, gardens, trees and flowers everywhere. The lake was full of fish, ducks and other birds, canoes and small embarkations. It had taken the Spanish only three months--and countless battles, adventures and adversity--to get there after arriving on the coast.

As the Tlaxcalans had made clear that the impersonator was not Montezuma, the real Montezuma made his appearance, enrobed in feathers and a marvelous jeweled headdress, his ears and nose ornamented with jade. Cloaks were laid at his feet so he would never touch the ground, and his subjects lowered their eyes. Cortés was 34, Montezuma, whom he considered a boy--especially after his capture when he would break into crying jags, or when he would follow Cortés around with doglike fidelity-- was older by seven years.

Cortés and his men were provided with comfortable quarters and offered endless gifts. Cortés was astonished by the splendor surrounding the king. He had a thousand servants and daily virgins were brought to him for his pleasure. Three hundred dishes were prepared for him each day, from which he would take a single bite. He drank cocoa and smoked tobacco. He had an enormous menagerie with everything from jaguars to crocodiles, that he fed with the remains of human sacrifices. The market was thought to be visited by sixty thousand people daily, who could buy anything from medicinal herbs to butchered body parts.

Cortés and Montezuma were both mass murders, no matter what their reasons. Montezuma was responsible for the horrible deaths of thousands of innocent boys, and Cortés caused the deaths of hundreds of thousands killed through war and disease, like smallpox that some historians say was the real reason the Spanish finished by conquering the Aztecs. Cortés and Montezuma became, on the surface, fast friends. They picnicked in the woods, boated on the lake, played various kinds of games, often with dice, some Aztec games, some Spanish. Cortés would apparently cheat, sending Montezuma into paroxysms of laughter. The stakes were jewels, and what Cortés won he kept, what Montezuma won he gave to his captors, his captors because Cortés had made him an offer he couldn't refuse: remain with him as his guest or, as one of his lieutenants chimed in, ''Die like a dog.'' Hours passed in talk, Montezuma always trying to learn as much as he could about every aspect of Spanish culture and weaponry. Then one of Montezuma's sons returned from the coast where he had been sent on a secret punitive raid against the Spanish. Cortés requested that the boy be put in his hands for questioning, which Montezuma agreed to. The lad was tortured until he admitted that he had been responsible for the death of

Spanish soldiers, under the orders of his father. He and a score of chiefs were taken to a public square and burned at the stake, in front of Montezuma and the city's inhabitants. The sight and screams literally obliterated Montezuma. From then on nothing but the shell of the man remained. Like Pizarro with Atahualpa, Cortés obliged Montezuma to call in gold from every corner of his empire.

That Cortés could carry out such atrocities in the midst of a million city dwellers is a total mystery. But the force of his willpower was not only victorious against the Aztecs. Word came from the coast that 18 Spanish ships had arrived carrying five times the number of Cortés' troops. Cortés left Montezuma in the hands of a trusted lieutenant and went to meet the commander of the forces. He sent ahead gold to bribe those who could be bribed and, arriving at night in the midst of a deluge, he attacked the Spanish camp and succeeded in partially blinding and capturing the commander. Thanks to the bribes and his incomparable authority and verbal eloquence, he brought the new troops over to his side.

In the meantime his lieutenant, in the Aztec capital, learned that during an upcoming festival, the most important of the year, in which a virgin boy would have his heart cut out and displayed, still beating, to the sun, the Aztecs planned to capture the Spanish, imprison them, sacrifice them and then eat them. The cream of Aztec society, its nobles and its finest warriors, said to have been several thousand in number, gathered in a central square where, in the middle of one of their ceremonies, the Spanish massacred them all. They then returned to the palace and barricaded themselves in.

Cortés returned and made the fatal mistake of freeing Montezuma's brother who promised to negotiate a truce between Cortés and the Aztecs sieging the palace. Instead he deposed Montezuma, the first time in Aztec history, and continued the siege. After weeks of battle, with Cortés' men reduced to literally sucking black ground water from holes they made in the palace gardens, Cortés had Montezuma led to the roof where he was ordered to calm the Aztecs. Instead, he was pelted with stones. Three days later he died, from his wounds according to the Spanish, garroted say the descendants of the Aztecs (a rope was tied around his neck, a stick inserted, and then twisted).

What followed is known, in Spanish history, as *La Noche Triste*. Cortés decided to run for it. He had had the Aztec treasures in sculptures melted into gold bars. At midnight, after mass, he and his men bolted. While crossing the causeways they were sitting ducks, and although the Aztecs lost thousands, Cortés lost 600 of his men, and all the gold, now at the bottom of the lake surrounding the City of Dreams. Cortés' skull was fractured in two places, two fingers were crushed, and his body badly wounded. Many Spaniards had been left behind, wounded. They now had their hearts cut out and their flesh eaten. The Aztecs didn't follow those who made it to the jungles, a terrible mistake, for Cortés, armed with his courage and brain, would return to see most of them into an early grave, and their wealth flow into Spanish, Medici and Papal banks.

- 5 -

Caravaggio had made many friends when he first arrived in Rome and slept rough in the vicinity of the Campo Marzio. Not all the religious leaders gorged themselves on the pleasures of life, some religious orders existed that cared for the poor by offering food and medical care. Caravaggio arrived at a time of famine and literally may have escaped death by starvation. Thanks to the Colonna (who had employed his father and who would take a special interest in Caravaggio to his last days) he found a room with a Monsignor Pucci whom he called Monsignor Salad as that was the extent of his nourishment, in exchange for shopping and keeping the dwelling in order. Caravaggio was given additional employment by Lorenzo Siciliano, specialized in the heads of the ancients that he sold cheaply to those who wanted to decorate their homes with the portraits of the Caesars. It was here he met another painter, Mario Minniti, first his lover, then a friend, and finally a benefactor at the end of Caravaggio's life.

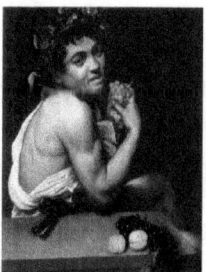

Sick Bacchus

With Mario he moved on to the workshop of Cavaliere d'Arpino (his real name Giuseppe Cesari) where he painted his *Sick Bacchus*, a self-portrait that gives one a queasy feeling as Caravaggio indeed looks deathly ill. D'Arpino was an arrogant tyrant who mistreated him, and if this and his illness were not enough, he was kicked by a horse and forced to spend several weeks in a free hospital, Santa Maria della Consolazione. He had placed some paintings with an art dealer, Costantino Spata, who sold one, the wonderful *Cardsharps*, to Cardinal del Monte who took him in. Cardinal Francesco Maria del Monte was a man known for his paternal interest in boys in general, and artists in particular, who introduced homoerotic art into the Vatican (just one of the reasons it is a must for every lover of art), and was himself homosexual. The palace housed as many as fifty boys, artists like Caravaggio, actors who took part in plays dressed as women when the role demanded it, rent-boys when out of work, and castrati. Caravaggio came with his luggage: a tormented mind, a character as unruly as his hair, violent fists and a sword and dagger at his side, despite their interdiction in the holy city famed for its bordellos, and, especially, Cecco. Rome's clergy lived in palaces and needed architects, sculptors and playwrights to fill their theaters, painters like Caravaggio, and warm bodies to span their nights. One Englishman described Italians as being addicted to ''the art of Epicureanism, the art of whoring, of poisoning and of sodomy.''

It's almost as if Caravaggio started his life writing comedies, and ended it with tragedies so intense as to make Edward Albee plays (like *Whose Afraid of Virginia Woolf*) resemble tales for children. The *Cardsharps* is all light and lightness, if one overlooks the knife that the boy cardsharp has at his waist, and the man looking over the innocent boy's shoulder, more menacing than the knife. The painting is of watershed importance as Caravaggio had left the comfort of d'Arpino's workshop for the cutthroat outer world, where his proclivity for life's dark side would see him into an early grave. The innocent boy in the painting is the kind that life has been kind to, offering him the best in clothes and the brightest of futures, unless, of course, the den into which he's stumbled decides otherwise. A boy lucky from birth, sitting opposite a lad knowing an entirely different destiny, having fallen into the hands of the Fagin looking over the guileless youth's shoulder. The expression in the man's eye is comical, yet, as one commentator succinctly put it, the man's eyeball is wide-open, staring and avid, yet seemingly out of control, which gives it a criminal intent. An amazing amount of emotion in a single gaze, proof again of Caravaggio's otherworldly talent. The man also has a black cloak, redolent of those who wished to pass through dark alleys at night, unseen.

Sold by the art dealer Costantino, the painting found its way to del Monte.

The idea of painting cardsharps turned out to be a genial inspiration because it was soon exploited by numerous other painters, especially de La Tour in his *Cheat with the Ace of Clubs.*

It was *The Cardsharps* that decided del Monte, a lover of boys, to invite Caravaggio to the Palazzo Madama, a decision that couldn't have been difficult given Caravaggio's evident talent and the beauty of his lover Cecco, both invited to share a small room in the palazzo.

Today the origin of the painting is in dispute as some experts believe it to be a copy. It was sold by an auction house in 2006 as a painting ascribed to a 17th century follower of Caravaggio for around £50,000. As it is now evaluated at over £10,000,000, a lawsuit was brought against the auction house for misattribution. The buyer, dead at age 100, ordered that it be perpetually on public view, which is the case as today it is in the Museum of the Order of Saint John in London, in honor of Caravaggio's having been made a Knight of Saint John on Malta.

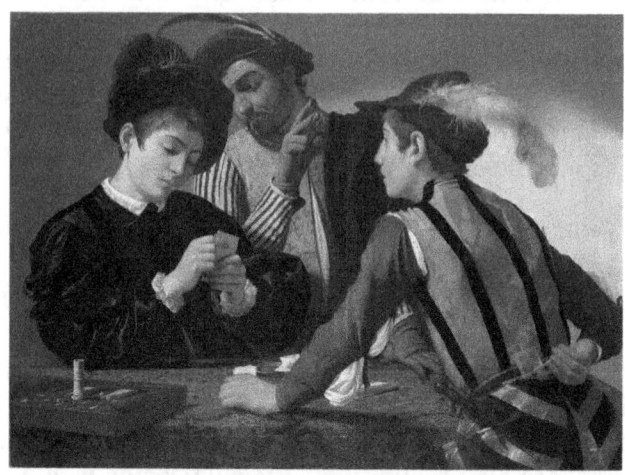

The Cardsharps

- 6 -

One of his early biographers, Giovanni Bellori, describes Caravaggio as being dark, dark in his looks, in his temperament and in his art, all of which is true. Another description of Caravaggio's place in Rome and Roman violence comes from Tommaso Garzoni, relayed to us by Graham-Dixon: "Every day, every hour, every moment, they talk of nothing but killing, cutting off legs, breaking arms, smashing somebody's spine ... For study, they have nothing other than the thought of killing this or that person; for purpose, nothing more than to avenge the wrongs that they have taken to heart; for favor, nothing more than serving their friends by butchering enemies..." With Caravaggio we will continually go from summit to summit, one in blazing light--that of his art, the other in princely dark--his intimate nature. Caravaggio was Alex in *Clockwork Orange.*

He soon came to know his fellow artists against whom he fought for commissions, all of whom lived in the same vicinity, ate in the same restaurants, drank in the same taverns, and bought their supplies from the same street vendor, Antinoro Bertucci. Caravaggio started out, as said, by painting the heads of famous early Greeks and Romans, very popular among those climbing the ladder in society, exchanging their mercantile or militaristic origins for those of the educated nobility. From there

Caravaggio went on to still lifes, another field just opening up, one he would combine, later on, in his paintings of young shirtless boys, like the *Boy with a Basket,* holding or surrounded by flowers and fruit.

Caravaggio's first paintings were full of light and eroticism, and *The Boy with a Basket* is sublimely sensual and joyful in the sense that the boy on the canvas was Caravaggio's lover, Mario Minniti, perhaps around age 16--what the Greeks considered the divine age (7), and what is appealing is that they were both young, both in Rome for the first time, both experiencing the ups-and-downs inherent in life but, being young, they were armed against all eventualities, armed by their youth, although they certainly didn't realize it due to moments of real hunger, thirst and despair, not knowing, in the early years, where they would sleep rough that night, yet they had life's greatest gift, each other.

So Mario posed as the *Boy with a Basket,* the painting sold by the street dealer Costantino at the Piazza San Luigi dei Francesi and bought by del Monte--the rest, as they say, is history.

The fruit is what we find in all of Caravaggio's work, so real a fly could attempt to land on the moldy grape or the moist interior of the pomegranate or the slightly rotting skin of the apple. The perfection continues in the skin of the boy, the folds of his garment, the weave of the basket.

The boy has the come-hither look of seduction, his shirt carelessly exposing his shoulder, his hair tousled, a reminder of bed, accentuated by heavy bedroom eyes, the most erogenous part, in this picture, of Mario's body.

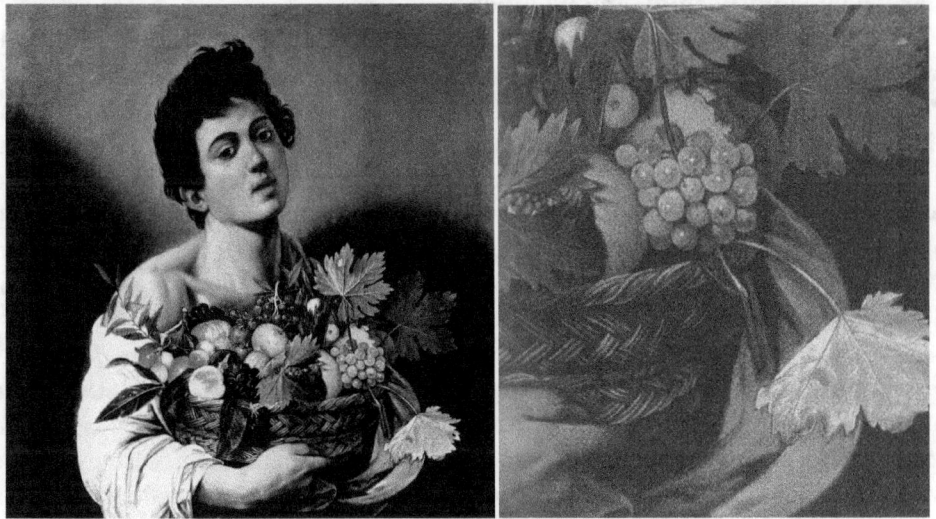

The sublime Mario Minniti in *The Boy with a Basket* and detail.

Del Monte was a cardinal in the service of Ferdinando de Medici who lent him the Palazzo Madama. He earned a good salary but had no personal fortune. His brother was a famous mathematician who had taught Galileo. Del Monte lived for art and the collection of art, surrounded by boys who executed his every wish, but he was known for his modesty and modest lifestyle, eating and dressing frugally--even shabbily said some--and was deeply religious (which never ever stilled sexual ardor).

He was nonetheless a friend of Giulio Mancini, an atheist, Caravaggio's biographer and part-time art dealer who sold several of Caravaggio's works. He was also a physician, in the service of del Monte and Caravaggio. At his death he left a fortune to the students of Siena where he'd been born.

The Boy with a Basket came into the possession of Scipione Borghese. The importance of Scipione Borghese to us is the combination of several factors: Born Scipione Caffarelli he was turned over to Camillo Borghese, the future Pope Paul V, because his father, fallen on hard times, didn't have the funds to educate and bring him up in a noble manner. Paul V changed the boy's name to Borghese and made him a cardinal and his secretary. Scipione guarded the door to the pope, thanks to which he amassed an immense fortune, making him perhaps the wealthiest man in Rome. (His ''salary'' alone, for 1612, was 140,000 scudi, while François I offered Cellini a yearly stipend of 300 scudi, which gives one an idea of what Scipione was worth.) To these factors were added his gift of extreme intelligence and passion for art and the collection of art, turning the Palazzo Borghese into an incomparable museum, while assuring the material comfort of Caravaggio and Bernini, among others.

Against Paul V's wishes, Scipione brought his lover Stephen Pignatelli to Rome and together they filled the palazzo Borghese with homoerotic art. Pignatelli was said to have loved Scipione to the point of insanity. Both men shared the services of other boys, one of whom, age 18, they were thought to have ordered murdered, just outside their bedroom, perhaps because the boy had sought bribes to keep Scipione's tendencies from his uncle the pope. Pignatelli was requested to leave Rome but was brought back when Scipione became deathly ill, and only his lover's presence could heal him. Scipione immediately recovered and was awarded a cardinal's hat.

Amusingly, Scipione commissioned Bernini to sculpt a *Hermaphrodite*, a reclining figure with an ample appendage, found today in the Louvre, the backside to the public. In order to view the statue's singularity, one has to squeeze between the pedestal (and wonderfully sculpted mattress over which the Hermaphrodite reclines) and a wall, which only people who know what to look for do (at least that was the logistics a number of years ago when I viewed it).

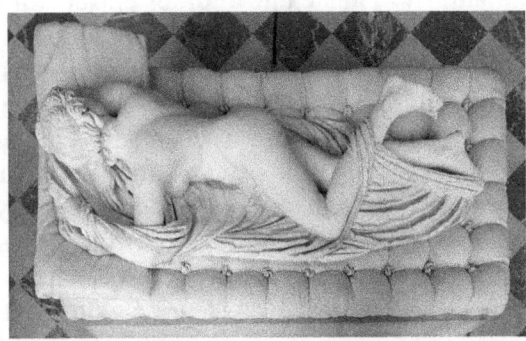

The Sleeping Hermaphrodite with full erection, the Louvre.

Paul awarded Scipione 105 paintings confiscated from the artist Cavaliere d'Arpino to cover unpaid taxes. The pope also stole Raphael's *The Deposition* from the Baglioni Chapel in Perugia, gave it to Scipione, and then legalized the theft with something called the *motu proprio* which somehow made what a pope did lawful.

Caravaggio spent several years in the Palazzo Madama. His quarters were extremely small but he was clothed and feed. Del Monte seemed to have been friendly but rigorous, far from the intellectual, easygoing Lorenzo *Il Magnifico*. Contrary to what I've written above about del Monte's modesty, one source states that his servants wore caps when serving him at table, ordered to raise them every time del Monte took a drink, a far cry from *Il Magnifico* whose dinners were excuses for friends to come together for free-reining conversations. Yet Caravaggio's years with del Monte were certainly the most stable and uncomplicated of his existence.

– 7 –

He had boys for his bed, especially Cecco whom he had known as a child and who had grown into an exquisite young man. Sodomy was punished by death, but as it was practiced as often in Rome as in Florence, rare were the persons tried for the crime, rare, at any rate, among the nobility and, even more, among the clergy. But an artist kept his lusts a secret as his commissions could suffer with this kind of taint to his reputation. Of course, none of this stopped Caravaggio who at all times satisfied his sexual lust and his lust to fight. He attacked a young man, a notary, from behind as he walked along the Piazza Navona, in plain daylight, because the boy had somehow insulted him, perhaps over one of Caravaggio's girls. Profusely bleeding, the boy got to the police to tell his story, before rushing off, unaided, to the hospital. The painter wound up paying a large indemnity. Then came another episode in a restaurant where Caravaggio had ordered some artichokes, half cooked in oil, half in butter. When he asked the server which was which, the lad answered that he had only to smell them to find out. Caravaggio took this as arrogant disrespect and hit him with the porcelain plate used to serve the artichokes, severely cutting him. He then reached for his sword but the boy had the presence of mind to bolt. Here too he had to pay up. Stopped by a policeman for carrying a sword, he had, exceptionally, a permit to do so on him (permits given to high officials and their bodyguards). The policeman bid him ''Goodnight,'' but as he walked away Caravaggio, perhaps unhappy that an artist like himself, who knew so many great men, had been detained by a redneck officer, called him, to his back, a cocksucker, and invited the gentleman to shove his ''Goodnight'' up his bloody ass. He was thrown in jail but was released the next day, as he knew he would be.

Caravaggio was far from the only man in Rome with murderous instincts. Even a terrible flood that left 1,500 dead couldn't keep all Rome from being stunned by a murder among the nobility, that of Count Francesco Cenci by his coachman--his daughter's lover--Catalano, who bludgeoned him with a hammer. The count had at first been drugged by his daughter, Beatrice, assisted by her stepmother, the count's wife Lucrezia, whom Count Cenci repeatedly raped in front of Beatrice. His sons, Giacomo and Bernardo, were in on the plot, as the count had tried to sodomize them too, as well as having incest with Beatrice. (She's thought to have had a child, but from her father or the coachman is unknown.) The murder was camouflaged as an accident by shoving the count's body over the broken railing of his palazzo. It was the murder of the century and even Pope Clement wanted to be kept continually up-to-date. If this weren't enough, a Cenci cousin, Paolo di Santa Croce, killed his mother when she refused to bequeath him her estate. The pope could understand murder to ensure one's inheritance. What he wanted were details concerning Cenci. He knew the Cenci were part of Rome's most ancient aristocracy. Cristoforo Cenci had worked for the Papal court and had amassed a fortune in mansions, farms and palaces, all of which he left to his son Francesco at his death, when the boy was twelve. His mother couldn't control her son who attacked servants at the slightest provocation, shedding blood and accumulating lawsuits. Even at age twelve he tried to bend male and female servants and stable boys to his sexual will, and contented himself, his hand always down his trousers, when the palace help and courtesans that he was already frequenting were unavailable. His mother married him off at age fourteen to a girl the same age. His own children soon followed, among whom were Giacomo, Cristoforo, Rocco, Bernardo and Beatrice.

His sexual attacks on the palace servants continued, with his being forced to pay up when he lost suits, although on one occasion he was able to get a boy hung thanks to false witnesses in his pay. Accusations against him were usually based on brutality, fornication and sodomy. On occasion he was imprisoned, earning his freedom only by shelling out what amounted to tens of thousands of scudi. A period of instability then followed when one dead pope was replaced by another in rapid succession. Criminality and debauchery reigned supreme, a perfect climate for Cenci whose physical and sexual violence continued unchecked.

His wife died in childbirth and he took another, Lucrezia, whom he raped when she was unwilling to have sex, rapes that took place in front of his daughter Beatrice, all the while continuing to sodomize his stable hands. Cenci was finally brought to trial for sodomy and found guilty. By paying 100,000 scudi, a colossal sum, to the Papal Exchequer, he escaped being burned at the stake.

Cristoforo and Rocco, following in their father's steps, were both killed in duels over whores, and Cenci retired to a mountain palace retreat accessible with difficulty even by mule with Lucrezia and Beatrice. The palace retreat was looked after by an extremely handsome caretaker, Olympio Calvetti, who became Beatrice's lover. Cenci returned to Rome, leaving the two women virtual prisoners. When he returned it was to continue the rape of his wife and of his daughter.

Finally Beatrice convinced her stepmother and her lover Calvetti to rid them all of Cenci. Calvetti enlisted the help of a friend, Marzio Catalano, and together they entered Cenci's bedroom and bludgeoned the sleeping figure to death. Cenci was then pushed from the palace balcony. The protective balustrade was later broken so as to appear an accident.

Cenci's sons, Giocomo and Bernardo, returned from Rome, although neither they nor Lucrezia and Beatrice took part in Cenci's burial, which got people talking to such an extent that an enquiry was made. Calvetti's wife, jealous that her husband had had a child with Beatrice (unless it was her father's) told the investigators that she had seen her husband destroy the balustrade *after* Cenci had fallen. Marzo, too, soon admitted his role in the affair. It came out that Giocomo, in Rome, had known about the assassination plans, but Bernardo had not.

Cenci's body was exhumed and it was found that his ghastly wounds could not have been caused by a simple fall.

At the trial the people of Rome were in favor of Beatrice when the details of her ordeal came out, and Giacomo and Bernardo testified that Cenci had tried to sodomize them. But the pope and the nobility had no desire whatsoever to see any of them escape punishment, as that would open the doors for their own assassination at the hands of disgruntled children and servants.

Lucrezia and Beatrice were accompanied by so many thousands to their place of execution, all wailing the coming death of the two martyrs, that segments of the crowd fell into the Tiber and were drowned. Both were beheaded. Giacomo and Calvetti were paraded through the streets while red-hot pinchers pulled flesh from their bodies. At the execution site both were bludgeoned to death, their bodies cut to pieces and hung on hooks

Innocent little Bernardo was informed that he would suffer the same fate. He was obliged to witness the executions of all four before being told he would only be obliged to man the pope's galleys until his death, which those in the know knew to be worse than death itself. The pope was given the details, and was satisfied.

– 8 –

After this we discover another chapter in Caravaggio's dark existence. Ranuccio Tomassoni had a stable of women he put on the streets. Known for his extreme good looks and for being well-endowed, his women were jealous of whom he chose to bestow his favors, to the point of attacking one another with daggers, hoping to scar a pretty face, or splash it with acid. The Roman police were called in numerous times to bring calm to the domestic situation. Ranuccio was always armed despite its unlawfulness, but invariably defended himself by stating that in his business being armed was necessary due to the girls' rowdy clients. At the same time, it appears that Caravaggio might also have had girls who disputed their places on the streets with those of Ranuccio, the basis of an explosive situation that would lead to Caravaggio's attempt to knife the boy, perhaps aiming at his genitals but striking instead the femoral artery, a place certain to cause nearly instant death. Both Caravaggio and Ranuccio had been accompanied by three men each. Onorio Longhi was there on Caravaggio's side and a captain of the guards was with Ranuccio. The captain too was run through but whether he died or not is uncertain. Caravaggio was put out of action with a blow to the head. The surviving six men stated that the incident had been over an unpaid wager on a tennis match although, most probably, it was a duel over prostitution, but as dueling in Rome carried the death sentence. Caravaggio fled before his trial and was therefore sentenced to death. A bounty was put on his head, a head that could literally be presented, severed from the body, in order to claim it.

Other sources give slightly different versions of Ranuccio's character. In one version Ranuccio Tomassoni was described as a sweet bird of youth whose innocence was cut short by a fatal sword blow to the boy's private parts, a deliberate attempt by Caravaggio to emaciate the virginal lad. Others have him as a well-hung pimp whose girls vied with each other for his charms, turning tricks with the view of the boy's bedding them as recompense for the girls' putting out.

Concerning Caravaggio, he is painted as a troublemaker--which no one could deny--but one who simply found himself in the wrong place at the wrong time. Others maintain that he was fucking Renuccio's favorite whore, or, in still another, Caravaggio was trying to get Renuccio's whores to work for him.

One thing is nonetheless certain, Caravaggio used whores like a certain Fillide for his models, the reason for which his Madonnas and Magdalenas were banned from churches and chapels by priests, and why he had to forgo commission after commission when it became known that he used them. (Even so, a painting refused by a church was instantly snapped up by a private buyer, often at far higher prices, and those accepted by priests often found their value quadrupled nearly overnight.) But the models, whores or not, were most often gorgeous, possessing a virginal aura known normally only to nuns.

It was for the bodies of these women that Caravaggio and Tomassoni may have had their dispute, and Caravaggio aiming at the lad's groin may have been in jealousy, as the girls certainly filled him in on the boy's dimensions and sexual prowess. It's not impossible, too, that Caravaggio lusted for the lad who preferred his girls, girls who would literally maim each other, attempting on more than one occasion *sfregio*, the cutting and disfiguring of an opponent's face, instantly ending her sexual appeal.

Carrying a sword in Rome could be punished by death, as reported. Dueling was not only punishable by death, the punishment was often truly carried out as a desperate means of stopping this most-favored form of rendering justice.

Details of what had taken place surfaced, later, and became known to the public, which are these:

In testimony given before the authorities, the witnesses to the feud between the sweet-boy/pimp and the acclaimed artist/jealous-avenger claimed that there had certainly not been a duel, that the lads were exchanging words when one of them--not specified--refused to honor a wager of 10 scudi at the end of a tennis match (whether a match between themselves or others they had both bet on, is unknown). The words led to the mysterious apparitions of weapons (weapons they had certainly not been carrying), followed by an accidental blow from which Ranuccio was wounded in the upper thigh. Caravaggio's sword had been seized by a friend of Ranuccio who hit Caravaggio over the head with it, knocking him cold. Ranuccio's brothers were captains in the guards, known for their brawling, their swaggering dominance over every back alley in Rome, their drinking, their swordplay and their predilection for humping their brother's whores. Horny stuff, in an era where power made everything right. Caravaggio, too, had his boys, Onorio Longhi, arrested time and again for every possible misdemeanor (although, following Caravaggio's death, Longhi would straighten himself out enough to become an architect of churches, followed by his son, another architect). Minniti may have been there, Caravaggio's long-time bedmate, who would also turn out straight in the sense that he would eventually marry, twice, father children, and mount a workshop that would flood Sicily with works of art, some of which were of true artistic value.

Now on the run, Caravaggio left Rome with all that was precious to him, his clothes and painting materials, his money and Cecco. He went to the Palazzo Colonna where he begged Constanza Colonna, whom we met at the beginning of our story, for help, help immediately offered as he and Cecco were packed off to the Colonna estate in the Alban Hills. There he painted *David with the Head of Goliath*.

Interlude

David with the Head of Goliath (second version)

This was a second version of *David with the Head of Goliath*. In this version David seems less stricken, less soulful for the killing of Goliath. David takes the head to Saul, the first king of Israel, soon succeeded by David himself after the deaths of Saul's sons and Saul's own suicide to escape his enemies. David carries his sword over his back, in this version, as one might a fishing pole, a warrior become again the boy he still is. The boy is Cecco, and we can rejoice that man and boy, Caravaggio and Cecco, still have each other.

The painting was bought by Juan de Tassis, Count of Villamediana, and taken to Spain. Juan's father was an ambassador of Philip III. A poet, Juan was described as being everything from arrogant to vain, intelligent to obscene. Juan offended the wrong people with his gossip and satirical writings--especially his claim to be fucking the queen, King Philip's wife--making enemies who would finish by assassinating him as he stepped from his carriage in Madrid. The public knew Juan as being an insatiable womanizer, but in private he was known for his preference for men, for his assiduous frequentation of both homosexual and heterosexual brothels, and, indeed, his autopsy presumably uncovered clear signs of anal activity. Presumably.

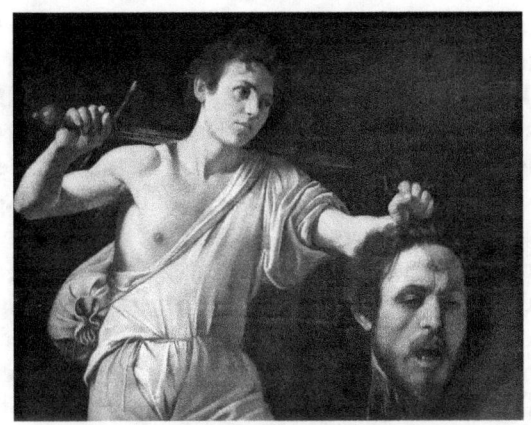

David with the Head of Goliath

CHAPTER FOUR

THE SCANDAL OF THE CENTURY: PERKIN

In other chapters I recount, as precisely as possible, the intellectual and political settings for the artists, like Caravaggio, who have left so many wondrous stars in our midst. We can never be grateful enough for men such as Cosimo de' Medici for bringing in the Renaissance thanks to the uncovering of texts from the Sun of all these stars, our hollowed ancestors the Greeks. I've tried to bring back the lives of Cosimo and his grandson *Il Magnifico*, leaders like the Sforza, Alexander VI and Julius II, Cesare and Catherina de' Medici. In this chapter we'll discover Edward IV and Henry VII of England, and the role of the scum who took the lives of two innocents, Richard III. We'll discover Margaret of Burgundy. We'll uncover the stories of two lads, so unique, so incredible that their existence is believed only because we have the facts locked away in documents: Simnel and Perkin.

The story of Simnel and Perkin is as true as one can make it after half a millennium. It's a passionate tale that involves five very lonely people: A boy who lost his father and his brother, and was himself purportedly assassinated at age 9: Richard, son of Edward IV. A tale of another lad, abandoned young to his destiny, whose love of beautiful clothes--a setting for his own beauty--would lead to the loss of his beautiful head, a lad born with the name Perkin. A woman, Margaret of Burgundy, wife of Charles the Bold and sister of King Edward IV and Richard III, whose only request of life was the birth of a baby she would never bear, but who found her consolation in adopting two other lads, two pretenders, Simnel and Perkin. A king, James of Scotland, whose father died in war and who spent his childhood seeking another. And, finally, a king marked by the loss of his father at an early age, a king who fought tooth and nail for a kingdom and won it thanks to the death of the boys in the Tower, King Henry VII.

Richard, Duke of York, second son of Edward III, and his brother Edward were smothered by their uncle, their father's brother, Richard III, in the most vile murder England has known, the murder of two children. Little Richard and his brother Edward V had been locked in the Tower of London. As Edward was the older he guessed the fate awaiting them both, and despite Richard's trying to entice him into play, he grew each day more saturnine. When the end did come, in the midst of the night, it was Edward who was thankfully asleep, while Richard, seizing immediately the purpose of the men who stole into the boys' chambers, begged them to take him and permit his brother the king to live. The assassins took both. Richard III was later killed in battle, his soul brought to rot each time one opens Shakespeare to read of his dastardly deed, the robbing of two boys of their precious lives.

Perkin, the boy who would be chosen by Yorkists to replace the smothered Richard, was spotted, in Ireland, during a festival on which the usual sumptuary laws did not apply. Decked out in superb doublet and beautiful black gown, news of his beauty and countenance brought his attention to those who wished to undo the King of England in favor of the Yorkists, in battle against the Lancastrians for generations. The boy refused his being taken for royalty, refusal upon refusal until the awe and respect of those who had approached him--he whose parents had set him on his own like a wandering gypsy from childhood--gradually succumbed to their impressments. The task was herculean in its vastness: He would have to learn manners and princely comportment. He would need the Latin learned as a child by the real Richard and the English language the real Richard had spoken since birth. He would need to know the daily lives of his father, King Edward IV, and his mother, as well as those of their advisers and his and his brother's servants. He would need to know his daily routine from the moment he awoke to the moment he retired.

It was the sitting king, Henry VII, who would have to unmask the lad, a lad already accepted by the French king Charles VIII who was about the same age and who received the boy at his court and shared his mistresses with him, no big affair for Charles who prided himself on never having the same woman twice, even if he was the most ugly monarch in living memory. The lad was recognized by the Roman Emperor Maximilian and his son Philip, also about the same age as the pretender, and on friendly terms with him.

Henry VII was the monarch who founded the Tudors, ending--with the death of Richard III at Bosworth--the War of the Roses that had bled England white for generations. He would impose 24 years of relative peace, followed by his son Henry VIII. He married Edward IV's daughter

Elizabeth, unifying his red rose to her white rose. An act of genius immediately followed. He declared himself king a day *before* the Battle of Bosworth, thus allowing him to proclaim that those who had fought against him had been traitors, allowing him to confiscate their lands, castles and their goods. Then, after his coronation, he decreed that any of the traitors who would swear fealty to him could have their possessions back. Edward IV had had two bothers, Richard who became Richard III, now dead, and Clarence. Clarence had been convicted of treason and executed. But Clarence had a son, Edward, a possible threat to Henry VII because of blood more noble than Henry's. He was put away in the tower. Later Edward would share his cell and his bed (a usage of the times) with Perkin, and plot with the boy to overthrow Henry VII. For this Edward would be beheaded.

The plot thickened when a lad named Simnel appeared to claim that he was Edward, Clarence's son. As the real Edward was being held in secret, a prisoner in the Tower, no one could dispute his claim.

No one knows Simnel's real name, but around age 10 he was taken under the wing of a priest, Richard Simon, who decided to make the handsome boy a king. At first Simon decided that the boy would be Edward IV's son Richard, especially as their ages matched, but then switched to Edward, Clarence's son. The priest Simon was exceedingly erudite and taught the boy everything he would need to know about courtly behavior. Simon contacted Yorkists who found in Simnel the perfect tool to overthrow Henry VII. They began by spreading the rumor that Edward had escaped from the Tower and made his way to Dublin. It was in Dublin that Simnel was crowned King Edward VI (Edward IV's son, killed in the Tower by Richard III, had been Edward V). An army was mounted and various Yorkists went to Burgundy where Margaret of Burgundy, Edward's aunt, held power. She furnished 2,000 men who returned to England and met Henry's troops at the Battle of Stoke Fiend where they were defeated. Those not killed were executed except for Simons, saved due to his being a priest, although he was imprisoned for life. Incredibly, Henry felt that Simnel himself had been nothing more than a lad manipulated by adults. He made the boy a spit-turner in the royal kitchen, and later a falconer! The boy married and fathered a priest who exercised under Henry VIII.

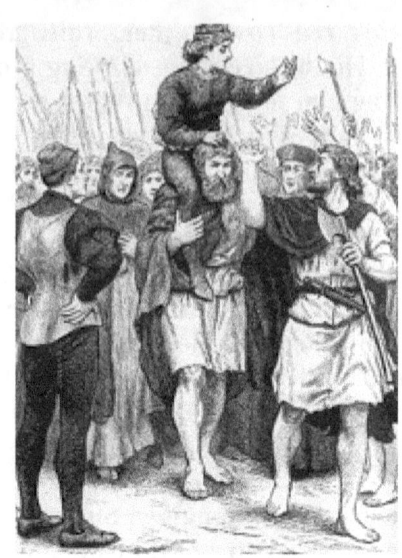
Simnel

What happened next was stranger still. A lad by the name of Perkin Warbeck (among other names, but we'll stick with that one, although from the age of about 17 onwards he'll be known to one and all as the boy who pretended to be Richard, the younger of the two lads imprisoned and executed by Richard III, and so I, too, will call him Richard until his capture by Henry VII). His mother supposedly sent him to Antwerp to learn Dutch and from there he was taken on by merchant ships that may have taken him as far as Portugal. But eventually he turned up in Ireland where his love of sumptuous clothing brought him to the attention of Yorkists who convinced him to play the role of the smothered Richard, as mentioned. From Ireland he went to Margaret of Burgundy, sister of Edward IV and Richard III, who wanted the Yorkists back on the throne with such intensity that she undertook the education of Perkin, as she had done with Simnel. He learned the ways and the secrets of the court of England, and his aptitude for languages and personal beauty did the rest. Margaret sent him to James of Scotland.

What followed next can only be described as a love affair between Richard and King James IV, a true love affair, albeit not necessarily in a physical sense because we do know that both Richard and James were ardent lovers of the opposite sex. Richard had wandered through Europe as a child and his early adolescence had taken place in Portugal and the royal court of Portugal, known for its liberality in matters sexual, and the ardor of its boys and girls in sharing of their bodies. James was insatiable, sexually, as were so many males of position throughout Europe, satisfying himself with the girls--from servants to courtesans to ladies of royalty--who expected and desired his attention. The same was true of France, as Henry

VIII was to learn thanks to Anne Boleyn and her sister, whom Henry had "known" long before Anne, girls brought up in the French court. Fingers, tongues and back passages were of no secret to even the youngest demoiselles in France and Portugal, while still maintaining an intact hymen. Boys adored ornamenting themselves in skin-tight trousers, leaving nothing of their muscular buttocks to the imagination, and, in front, held in place by strings or buttons, were cod pieces of immense dimensions, as alluring to maidens as were the boys' gestures, their hands stroking the immense bulges.

As so often with boys at that time, James had lost his father to battle when very young, and literally went from man to man, afterwards, with the heart-breaking question, "Are you my father, sir?" Richard (Perkin warbeck) had been set free from his father far too young, as had Henry VII whose father died in battle even before his birth. These men were drawn to their own through an absence that nothing in the world, nothing but one's only true father, can fill. This indelible emptiness was felt even when a father was physically alive but physically absent, called away, perhaps, by war, or simply not present to assuage the needs of his boy. This was the case with Maximilian whose father, the Roman Emperor Frederick III, lived to old age but was away at war, during which his son Maximilian had at times to beg for bread. Rare were those like Cellini to have a dad who desired a son more than life itself, and when presented with the precious gift loved him insatiably, naming him *Benvenuto*, Benvenuto Cellini (6).

James, at 22, was just a few months older than Richard. From the moment of Richard's arrival James took him in hand, literally in hand in the sense that at every possible occasion, and especially in church, James entwined his hands in those of Richard, hands they joined in the worship and the presence of God. They ate together, perhaps not from the same plate as Richard Coeur de Lion and Philippe II, and they slept in the same bed, without the intimacy of the young and futures kings of England and France--Richard Coeur de Lion and Philippe--but in a tradition even known to President Lincoln, and common in the American Far West. (As the time were omnisexual, it's of course conceivable that they may have been lovers.)

James was generous to a fault and far from rich, but Richard had nothing. After the mass, it was James who would make a contribution in the name of his friend. James was an athlete, but too trusting, as even his closest advisor, John Ramsay, was a spy in the pay of Henry VII. He was so concerned about his people that he would roam the countryside dressed as they, and seek lodging for the night amidst the most humble, all in an effort to learn what they thought of their king.

And lastly, James provided for his guest's needs by giving him the daughter of the wealthiest man in Scotland, Katherine Gordon, daughter of the Earl of Huntly. She was young, beautiful and virgin, and James saw to it that the marriage took place rapidly so that Richard and she could enter into union. Later, a captive of Henry VII, Perkin was denied access to Katherine, the reason for his ill-considered actions, while Henry lusted for her but apparently did not take advantage of his limitless powers. James and Katherine would remain loyal to the boy to the end, even if James was forced to make certain concessions to Henry in order to save his country.

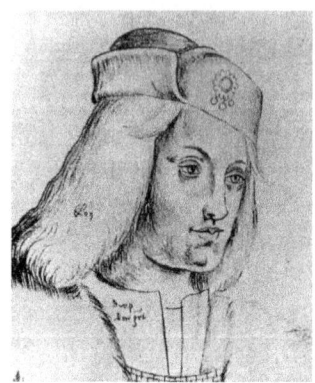
Perkin Warbeck

James and Richard recognized in each other the brother neither had ever had, the shared resemblance of two boys of the same age, the need of masculine affection that no woman can ever fulfill in a man, the reason men defend each other to the death in war, the indestructible nature of friendship we find in today's Australia where a man would die for his mate.

Naturally, everyone thought that with Richard on the English throne they could, one and all, gain something of priceless value with Richard in power: Margaret would have more say in the running of her Burgundy. The Roman Emperor Maximilian would have an English ally he could order around, as he could no longer do even his son Philip. And James would enjoy increased trade and more fluid relations with his neighbor England. But all said and done, James' chief motivation may well have been the beauty of his friendship with the boy-who-would-be-king.

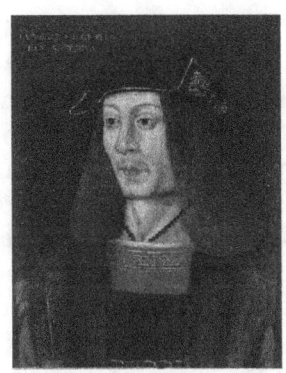
James IV

It was James who insisted on invading England, and Ramsay reported to Henry that James, who loved joists and fighting with axes and swords and crossbows, was pushing the boy forward. But Richard was not enthusiastic about an invasion because he *knew* the truth behind his right to the throne of England. And anyway, he had a new wife with lands and nobility and in September he would have a son. What was the chimera of England now to him? He most resembled the Trojan Prince Paris, ensconced with Helen, behind the impregnable walls of Troy. But like Troy, the Greeks were coming in the form of Henry VII.

One is nonetheless amazed by the backing Richard benefited from: Maximilian and Burgundy under Maximilian's boy Philip; Margaret capable of offering vast sums of money; and a huge number of Yorkists and other supporters, all furnishing troops, horses and finances. A great number of Yorkists from England sent their seals to Richard as proof of their adherence to his plan of conquest. Alas, the seals were intercepted and forwarded to Henry who had most of the men, the cream of English nobility, beheaded. Only the very young were spared, if imprisonment for life can be so judged. Some did buy their way out, others had been truly loved by Henry and it was they who had no chance of being pardoned. Also, the sums invested by Henry in his defense were absolutely colossal. This was especially painful to a man who was one of history's original misers, amassing the greatest fortune England had ever known, money that would go to his son Henry VIII, making the boy, already lucky in looks and lucky in advisors, the richest lad in the world--until the gods decided to tip the scales, although only at the very end of Henry VIII's miserable life.

On the sidelines of all of this were Ferdinand and Isabella, King and Queen of Spain, a couple who had loved each other the moment their eyes met. Their intelligence, in the sense of both brainpower and spies, was such that they knew the truth about the boy, and spent every hour trying to convince the world, and thereby avoid useless wars. They brought order to government, they saved Spain from bankruptcy, they reduced crime for the first time in the country's history, and, icing on the cake, they sent Columbus on an excursion that would double the surface of the known world and enrich it beyond the grasp of the imagination.

At age six Isabella had been promised to Ferdinand but later it was suggested that she marry Edward IV of England or his brother the future Richard III, killer of infants, she held strong to her desire to wed Ferdinand. An obstacle to their union was their consanguinity, yet this was overcome by the Spanish Cardinal Borgia, the future Alexander VI. Her brother the king nevertheless disapproved, forcing her to escape to the wedding site, Valladolid, where she was joined by and married to Ferdinand who had been disguised as a servant to avoid the king's army. When the king died she was crowned but for the first years she had to wage war against those who thought they had a better claim to the throne. Even Portugal invaded in an attempt to seize power. Her place finally became legitimized with the birth of a son.

Slavery was forbidden--hundreds of years before Lincoln--under Ferdinand and Isabella, but the interdict was little applied. The Inquisition was given full power and Jews were allowed three months to leave Spain with neither gold nor silver nor money nor arms nor horses. Half are thought to have converted, perhaps cosmetically. Muslims too were ordered to convert or get out.

Their daughter Joanna was married to the Roman Emperor Maximilian's son Philip, opening the door for Roman rule over Spain. Their youngest daughter Catherine married Henry VIII's brother but he died, supposedly before consuming the marriage. Catherine went to Henry VIII himself, sowing the seeds for the destruction of the Catholic Church in England.

At Isabella's death she was entombed in a sepulcher built by the Roman Emperor Charles V, the new Charles I of Spain, Joanna and Philip's son. Ferdinand followed her, in the same chapel, a few years later.

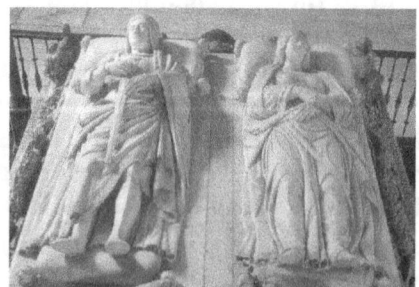

The tomb of Ferdinand and Isabella

James' plan seems to have been to cross the border into England, grab a few border towns, and thanks to the uprising of the English people--

especially Yorkists from the north--he would return home and let Richard continue on to glory. Before setting off, both friends had signed an agreement under which certain English lands and towns would be given to Scotland, and 100,000 marks forwarded to James' coffers once the lad was on the throne (which would have reimbursed a huge number of church donations James had offered in Richard's name).

The border was crossed and James initiated a burned-earth policy that left Richard in tears, claiming that James would leave him no one and nothing over which he could govern. Richard rode off to the safety of Scotland and as Henry's troops approached, James did likewise.

Following the collapse of James' army, Maximilian kept doggedly at Richard's side. Ferdinand and Isabella tried everything in their power to get the boy to Spain where they could pension him off, thereby neutering him. Maximilian's son Philip had long given up on the lad. Margaret had spent her last cartridges in his favor. Charles of France desperately wanted Richard as a joker to play in his wars with Henry. And Ireland took Henry's bribes and turned its back on the boy.

Henry's troops approached Scotland. Henry offered James his daughter, age 6, in marriage, a peace offering. Although Henry did not hesitate to put traitors to death, he had a very enticing side, one that had forgiven Simnel, had paid for his marriage and had set the boy up as a falconer. And despite the hundreds of deaths occasioned by Perkin, despite the cost in today's money of millions to Henry and a hunt that had gone on for six long years, despite all that Henry took the lad to his side, when finally captured, not as a son, but not far from being one either. And now here Henry VII was, offering his daughter, his own flesh and blood, to his enemy. But James refused to surrender his friend Perkin to what he believed was certain death. Yet as the wolves closed in on all sides, from Spain and especially from England, James had no choice but to ask his friend to leave, at the head of a small army, on an ill-named ship the *Cuckoo*, destination England where Richard would become king. No one was present at their goodbyes, but I hope they were worthy of the sincere love and wondrous moments they had shared.

But Richard was intercepted by Henry on the high seas and captured. Richard became Perkin.

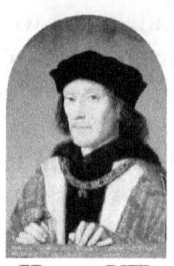

Henry VII

As I stated at the beginning of this chapter, this is a tale of five unhappy people. Henry VII had been an only son, his father dead before his birth and no noble men to show him the route to manhood, let alone kinghood. He had no real pedigree, no real royal blood, and until the rise of Henry VIII such would remain the case. Affable, he was nonetheless a loner and would stay so until the end of his life. Perkin Warbeck had stood alone from an early age, and the story of the conditions of his passing from one adult to another, as he passed from one country to another, will remain unknown, but was certainly trying and forlorn. His thirst for betterment was mirrored in his choice of clothes, which in turn brought him to the attention of others who would use him as he had always, in one way or another, been used. He lost to Henry but in so doing he gained a wife and child, was welcomed to Henry's court, one lonely man in the service of another, and there he could have risen to heights less than a kingly Richard IV, but to an unimaginable prosperity, given his lowly birth. It was perhaps Henry's own lowly birth, in comparison with other Yorkists and Lancastrians, that allowed him an intimacy--albeit limited--with humbler lads such as Simnel and Perkin. In his own gauche way he tried to make friends of them both, but it was the Fates, not men, the ultimate arbiters of one's destiny. Henry was 41, the boy, as he called him, 22. Perkin confessed all, totally astonished at the king's leniency. Maximilian and Margaret had known of the conspiracy, Perkin admitted to Henry, no one else knew, and certainly not James. On bended knee the boy confessed, but his manner was unweeping and noble. His wife was brought before Henry who was said to have lusted for her but had kept himself in check by sending Katherine to serve his queen, Elizabeth. Order had returned to the world, the planets again in their rightful orbits.

Maximilian requested Perkin's freedom. Philip turned his back on Perkin, provoking his father Maximilian to note the boy's willfulness and lack of cooperation. Katherine, bless her, remained faithful to Perkin, even after Henry had divulged all, but although Henry allowed them to meet at court, in public, he kept them separated physically, his way, perhaps, of unmanning the lad.

The power of fucking has always totally amazed and captivated me. Where along the evolutionary line did something available to nearly every living thing on the planet become an obsession, to such an extent that psychologists say a boy is no longer controllable once he has wet his brush, as the French say (*se tremper le pinceau*). The concept rules the locker room, occupying every thinking moment and expression between young men: "I made her cum three times last night." Even the word fuck itself is the ultimate in the English language. In the throes of orgasm it's cried out, as it is when a lad hits his finger with a hammer. Here Henry unmanned the boy Perkin by separating cock and cunt. At any rate, it was due to this deprivation that Perkin would attempt escape, and herald in his own death.

Perkin was free to roam the royal premises and the grounds, on foot or horse, accompanied by two unarmed guards that those not in the know took for his servants. Perkin was in fact so free of restraints that Henry had to defend himself by saying that the boy was indeed being punished, this to the obvious disbelief of those who had access to both men. Perkin slept in a small room near the king's and had a tailor paid by Henry. He was at court with Simnel, and one wonders if they were not looked down on, both just lowly fakes, after all, of lesser importance than the fire-eater or sword-swallower who, at least, both earned their keep through amusing the court. Perhaps they were both just tolerated because Henry tolerated them, and the king was the measure of all things. For Perkin, without his Katherine, the humiliation must have been unbearable.

All hell broke out when he escaped. The king offered 100 pounds for his capture, a huge sum. The reasons for Perkin's escape are unknown: A need to physically reunite with Katherine, hatred at being penned up and exhibited, or perhaps Margaret and Maximilian had offered him exile as a free man. Henry was said to have been indifferent, and even though the boy had tried to usurp his place, had cost him a fortune, and had been the cause of the loss of thousands of lives, this may have become the case.

He was caught four days later, totally undone, turned over by the monks from whom he had begged sanctuary. The end is painful to reveal. When Paris in Troy won a footrace, the crowds went wild in his favor because, said one, "the boy is young and beautiful and when offered the laurels, he wept"(4). Perkin too was young, just 23, and beautiful, but he lost, and as such he was put on exhibit before the people who spat on him. Few were those, like me, who had loved this boy for being the entirely unique lad who had kept the known world breathless: Ferdinand and Isabella who with every exchange of letters begged their ambassador to send more news of this Perkin; the Emperor of the Romans who dispatched a ship to his rescue the moment he learned of his flight; Charles VIII, King of France, jumping up and down with glee at Henry's embarrassment, beside himself with joy; and James of Scotland, on his knees before God whom he begged to save the life of his friend, unaware that God's chosen few had denied the boy sanctuary.

Contrary to popular belief, the Tower had more or less furnished rooms--the richness of which depended on the importance of the occupant--not cells. Perkin's was small, with a small bed, table and chair, and a window so small a single bar sufficed to make it escape proof. Some occupants had freedom of movement throughout the Tower. Perkin did not and may even have worn shackles and an iron neck collar. The cleanliness of the rooms, their salubriousness, depended too on the nobility of the inhabitant.

A delegation from Burgundy was sent by Margaret and Maximilian's son Philip in order to resolve certain questions between Henry and Burgundy, one of which was the health of Perkin, of upmost importance to Margaret. Ferdinand and Isabella's ambassador was invited to see the boy too, as the lad seems to have become an obsession to the Spanish, a kind of pop star whose every movement was of significance. Henry himself escorted the lot to Perkin's room. In front of them Perkin admitted that he was a fake, news to none present but something Henry insisted on during every visit by outsiders. The Spanish ambassador claims Henry had had the boy disfigured, that he had beaten the last remnant of beauty out of him. In public Henry expressed his disgust of Maximilian and James, and his utter hatred of Margaret, the mastermind behind the entire hoax, according to him. It seems that Margaret wrote to Henry, abjectly demanding his pardon.

The reader may remember that on gaining power Henry had imprisoned Edward, the son of Clarence, brother of Edward IV and Richard III. He had been imprisoned because he had had a better claim to the throne than Henry himself. Since then, plots unceasingly came to Henry's ears concerning Yorkists who dreamed of having Edward on Henry's throne. Other plotters wanted to place Perkin on the throne, as his right to it, as Edward IV's son, was far stronger than Edward's. It had become obvious, for years, that Henry would never know peace so long as both men continued to breathe.

We know that both Perkin and Edward shared their beds with guards who were there for the purpose of not leaving either man alone. These guards were also conveyers of messages from the outside so that at all times Perkin and Edward were aware of the plans to save them. Whether the guards were motivated by Yorkist loyalty or by gain or both depends on who recounts their stories. It is known too that the guards provided a human, comforting presence. The guards and Perkin and Edward were of the same age, young and virile. Perkin was age 24. Edward was age 24. Words and gestures of love between them were witnessed by others, sighs of lovemaking overhead, comforting solace that at the end neither Perkin nor Edward lacked for living presence and understanding.

Henry had his fortune told by a priest, a practice forbidden since Roman times. The priest foretold certain terrible events. Henry swore him to secrecy and then locked up everyone the priest spilled the beans to when in his cups.

The four guardians responsible for Perkin and the four responsible for Edward were accused of treason for conspiring to free the prisoners. They were hanged until nearly dead, disemboweled, quartered (literally cut into four pieces) and beheaded. Edward was found guilty of treason and, thanks to his nobility, only beheaded. After all, he had been the son of a brother to two kings. Perkin was found guilty and hanged with the aid of a ladder that was carefully withdrawn, allowing the noose to tighten and gradually bring death by strangulation, as long as an hour later.

This unique son of man ended his short journey on an earth wondrously bountiful, heartbreakingly beautiful and totally uncaring, having known vicissitudes well beyond those of mere mortals, having given of himself, having known the true devotion of a good woman and that of a loyal friend, having born a son, having brought love to the heart and tears to the eyes of the very lonely boy who is writing this, on his small boat, 500 years after the event, off the coast of France.

Interlude

The Boy Bitten by a Lizard

The boy in *The Boy Bitten by a Lizard* registers an expression of shock and surprise. Caravaggio apparently experimented on himself to obtain the expression, burning a finger while looking into a mirror to study his reaction. Indeed, some reviewers think the boy is a self-portrait of Caravaggio himself. Others believe him to be his lover, Mario Minniti, while still others believe this is not so as the boy is obviously effeminate, something that Minniti was not (although no biographer could possible know if Minniti had been effeminate). A rose in the ear, the hair made up like that of a geisha, and the loose shirt begging to be removed (says one reviewer) adds to the impression of an androgynous whore (states another).

The precision and absolute genius of Caravaggio is exemplified by the reflection of a distant window on the curved surface of the vase, as well as droplets of condensation (not visible, alas, in the enclosed reproduction). The rose is perfect, the cherries on the table are succulent and the boy's fingernails are grimy.

There exist two versions of the painting, both painted while Caravaggio, around age 21, resided with Cecco, at cardinal del Monte's palazzo.

The sexual symbolism escapes me personally, but at least one reviewer maintains that the cherries represent lust, the lizard the wounded penis, and the boy's surprise and pain his first butt-fucking. Other reviewers think that the boy's pain is symbolic of his discovery of pain in the world in general, light-years away from his being sodomized.

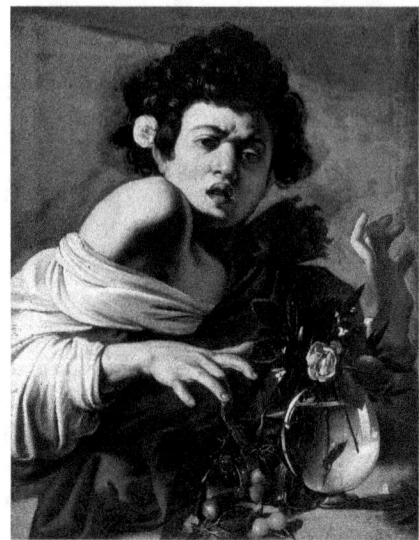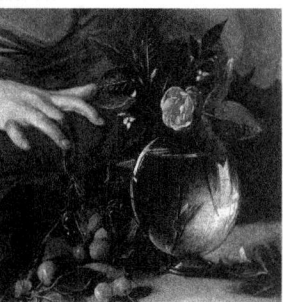

Boy Bitten by a Lizard and detail.

CHAPTER FIVE

MALTA

- 1 -

Caravaggio went to Naples, an immense city of 300,000, a decrepit city, home to criminals, crime and rackets, to the poor and scarcely educated, among whom labored 10,000 slaves. Yet the city thrived thanks to its sleepless citizens, scholars in trade, professors of import and export. As with Milan, Naples too was under Spanish rule, and as in ancient Rome, the nobility--meaning the Spanish and the wealthy--circulated through the streets in covered litters.

He resided with the Colonna but as his renown as an artist outshone his reputation for being a hoodlum, he did not need their help in securing what became a flood of commands. As in Rome, what could the rich do with their wealth, once their stomachs and loins were assuaged, other than tend to their palaces and gardens and interiors? But then word filtered through to Naples, from Rome, that Caravaggio had hired assassins to do away with his enemies, and whatever the truth of the matter, the uproar forced him to flee again, this time to Malta where thanks to the paintings he did for several Knights of Malta he gained near godlike admiration and was even knighted.

The wonderful adventures that predated the loss of Jerusalem in 1187, those of Richard Coeur de Lion of England and his lover Philippe II of France, continued on when the Knights of Saint John withdrew first from Jerusalem and then Acres, and sailed, in 1309, to Rhodes.

Also called the Hospitallers and the Knights of Saint John, the Knights of Malta began around year 1000 as an organization devoted to the poor and sick pilgrims who wished to visit the Holy Land. Attacks from Islamic forces gradually changed it into a military order recognized by the popes of Rome and dedicated to the physical protection of pilgrims.

Two hundred years later the Shadow of God on Earth, Suleiman, decided, in 1522, that Rhodes, 11 miles of the Ottoman coast, was a thorn that had to be extracted. He knew that the island was the best protected in all of the Mediterranean, with a thick-walled fortification created by the unequaled military engineer Gabrielle Tadini, a fortification that could produce its own gunpowder and was stocked to overflowing with grain. Numbering around 500 men from the aristocracy, wearing red cloaks bearing white crosses, the Knights were aided on Rhodes by local Greeks and mercenaries, all placed under the Grand Master Philippe Villiers de L'Isle Adam. Suleiman knew that Rhodes was powered by men limited in number, while his own were limitless clones, dispensable in the thousands.

His attack on Rhodes was greatly feared in Europe where Charles V said that should the Ottomans succeed "all of Christendom would be destroyed." Yet he and the pope and the other powers did nothing aside from dispatching 2,000 mercenaries that made it as far as the Bay of Biscay where storms drowned them all.

Sections of the fortifications on Rhodes were divided up according the nationalities. The Spanish wall was tunneled and blown up and Tadini received a ball in an eye socket that penetrated his skull, but he survived. The Knights built an inner wall and prayed that with the arrival of winter the Ottomans, as was their custom, would return home. But Suleiman continued the siege and even Tadini admitted that there was no way out. Incredibly, Suleiman let them leave with their possessions and arms and their most sacred relic, the arm of John the Baptist. Among those on the parting ships--only 180 out of the original 500--was Jean Parisot de La Valette, a Knight, and watching them go was a simple soldier called Mustapha. A man not on the ship was Tadini, kept back in service of the sultan. Seeing L'Isle Adam board his ship Suleiman said, "It's indeed sad to be obliged to throw this old man out of his home."

L'Isle Adam begged the rulers of Europe to give him a base where he could continue the Knight's war against the Ottomans. Henry VIII received him with honors and provided guns and power. Charles V gave him rocky, barren Malta. Charles had come to power at age 17. Suffering from inbreeding, his eyes bulged and his chin was so large his mouth hung open. An idiot in appearance, the inbreeding had not affected his brain. His son Philip would become King of England without speaking a word of English; Charles was King of Spain and knew no Spanish. His personal motto was *Further* and in all he accomplished, it fit him well.

The expulsion of the Moors from Spain fueled Suleiman's desire for revenge. He found the perfect arm for his fury in the Barbarossa brothers, first Oruch and then the younger Hizir. Born in Lesbos, their father was an Ottoman cavalry officer, their mother a Greek Christian. Oruch brought terror and barbarism wherever he attacked, but he himself was eventually cornered at Tlemcen by Charles' men. Fleeing on horseback, he sowed the trail with gold coins and jewels destined to slow his pursuers, a stratagem that didn't work on those who knew the immense price on his head. He had already lost an arm in a previous battle, and now the metal replacement was hacked off, along with his head, and his body was skinned and the skin nailed to the walls of Tlemcen.

His brother Hizir took up the torch, even dyeing his beard red like that of Oruch in order to perpetuate the fear of the Barbarossas. Hizir was given a fleet by Suleiman and proceeded up the coast of Italy to the town of Fondi north of Naples where he tried to capture Julia Gonzaga, countess of Fondi and unmatched beauty that Hizir wanted for Suleiman's harem. He succeeded only in killing hundreds of men and taking thousands of women and children as slaves back to Turkey, the boys to become future janissaries.

When Hizir captured Tunis Charles became frightened. Tunis was only a twenty-hour, 100-mile sail from his possession, the island of Sicily. A stepping-stone to Sicily was Malta, which Charles decided to fortify, at all costs, and who better to guard it than the warriors of God, the Knights of St. John?

But first he decided to recapture Tunis. He arrived with a fleet that took Barbarossa by surprise. Barbarossa ordered the thousands of Christian slaves in his possession killed, but their owners refused to turn their wealth into rivers of blood, and when the battle seemed to turn against the Ottomans, the slaves were released in the hope that they would save their owners, now their liberators. The freed slaves took weapons by storming an armory and, aided by Charles' soldiers, massacred every Muslim in sight before taking, for their own use, 10,000 prisoners. On his return to Naples a spectacular bullfight was organized in Charles' honor.

Barbarossa was thought to have perished in Tunis but he escaped and rounded up a fleet that he disguised as Spanish ships, ordering his men to shave. They entered Balearic ports, welcomed with shouts of joy. Those they didn't murder were sent to Africa where they glutted the slave market. Never was a beautiful girl or handsome lad cheaper to buy.

In his attempts to limit Charles' power, François I armed Barbarossa, providing him with guns, powder and cannonballs. He turned over France's natural port of Toulon. The Venetians too paid Suleiman ransom to spare the Serenissima, giving him their Mediterranean trading posts. When Barbarossa became too much of a burden, François was forced to pay him 800,000 gold pieces to sail out of Toulon, leaving the Toulonnais, who raised the sum, dirt poor but grateful. Barbarossa returned to Istanbul, sowing misery along the way, abducting thousands, especially men as rowers who shat in place and remained shackled and whipped until, weak, they were thrown overboard. Always, always the captured peoples found reasons to justify God's inaction in saving them. The island of Lipari is a case in point. The inhabitants agreed to pay for their freedom and in good faith allowed Barbarossa to land, after which he enslaved them anyway, seizing not only what the Lipariots were willing to pay but everything they had. To absolve God's absence it was said that the Lipariots were being made to pay for their proclivity to sodomy.

Barbarossa died of fever at age 80. His mausoleum on the Bosporus was visited by all departing naval expeditions as a sign of respect and to obtain his luck.

Charles V abdicated in 1550 and was replaced by his boy, Philip, King of Spain and the Holy Roman Empire, called the Prudent because, as opposed to his father, he was ever cautious. In fact it was said of him: If we have to wait for death let's hope it comes from Spain for it will never arrive. Charles entered a monastery to devote himself to God.

Like Charles, Suleiman was also old, 70, and he too was turning more and more to God. And it was herein the problem: Malta's new master, Jean Parisol de La Valette, the young Knight who had embarked at Rhodes, had ordered attacks on Ottoman ships. One ship so boarded--its occupants sold into slavery--had carried pilgrims from Mecca. If Suleiman could not protect God's followers, of what good was he? After the death of Barbarossa Suleiman had left the Mediterranean more or less at peace due to troubles at home: Persia was revolting, he had personally been present at the strangulation of his favorite son, accused of treason, only to learn later of the boy's innocence; another son had been murdered by his children, and the remaining son, Selim, was inept; there was corruption, uprisings among his janissaries, dissention among his viziers, and his favorite wife had just died; finally, famine and the Black Death plagued the land. He nonetheless realized that the thorn of Malta had to be extracted. At the same time,

Charles' boy Philip came to the conclusion that Malta was the key to the Christians' hold over the western Mediterranean. Suleiman decided to invade the island despite herculean difficulties. Whereas Rhodes had been in sight of Turkey, Malta was in sight of Sicily, just 30 miles away, but 800 miles from Suleiman's throne. Where Rhodes was fertile, on Malta there was nothing, not even a river, and water had to be collected in stone-carved cisterns. There were few places to invade along the cliff coast, with the exception of the magnificent bay in the hands of La Valette. Suleiman would have to bring absolutely everything necessary for an invasion aboard his own ships. The preparations were gigantic.

The Maltese were a mixture of every invading country that had ever passed that way: Greeks, Romans, Carthaginians, Phoenicians, Sicilians, among others. The Maltese spoke an *Arab dialect* and their word for God was *Alla*, but they had been converted by the shipwrecked Saint Paul himself, and were ardent Catholics. Like the Basques, they were one of nature's true mysteries.

The West had become aware of the coming invasion thanks to spies, but they had no idea of where it would take place. The Venetians feared for Cyprus, the Spanish for Sicily. But La Valette knew the truth. The destination was he himself. Like Charles, like Suleiman, he too was 70. Suleiman's fleet set off in a hurry in order to capture the spring winds, but too much in a hurry to parade before the mausoleum of Barbarossa, which would have assured their success.

La Valette had led a full life in the service of God since leaving Rhodes. He had fought innumerable battles, had been a galley slave for a year, as well as the governor of Tripoli. Wise, intelligent, versed in many languages, he would befriend Caravaggio and make him a fellow Knight, earning in return two major portraits of himself, one showing him with one of his many pages, his only supposed weakness.

The secret of Malta's defense was its natural harbor that penetrated the island to a distance of 4 miles, providing a series of inlets and islets, and offering superb anchorage and faultless shelter. The Knights' fortifications consisted of walls that prolonged the height of the cliffs, castles and three major forts, Saint Angelo, Saint Michael and Saint Elmo. As on Rhodes years before, the number of Knights was barely 600. These were aided by the superb Maltese, as well as a limited number of volunteers from other countries, especially Spain and Italy. Women and children were evacuated, although most Maltese chose to remain. La Valette wrote to Philip, his liege, and the pope, asking for help.

The Turks came with 130 galleys, 200 smaller vessels and 30,000 men. (Galleys were like Greek triremes, open rowing boats, not to be confused with ships, far bigger and basically powered by sails.) The Ottoman preparation for war was always faultless thanks to their incredibly efficient centralized bureaucracy, an enormous asset compared to irresolute Europe. The forces facing the Turks totaled 6,000. The Maltese were decided to fight until the last of their children.

The Turks landed and marched towards the fortifications, men dressed in bright clothing and carrying hundreds of flags and banners, accompanied by music, armed with swords and muskets. The defenders, armed with lances and harquebusiers, were so eager to leave the fort and fight under the red and white standard of St. John that La Valette couldn't give permission to open the gates fast enough. When the Knights withdrew into the fort at nightfall they left 500 enemy dead behind, having themselves lost 10 men. From then on La Valette, in order to save lives, allowed his men to fight from the top of the walls only (La Valette's 10 men could not be replaced, whereas 500 of Suleiman's men were a drop in the ocean of his reinforcements).

Hundreds of years of laying siege had made the Ottomans the most accomplished force on earth. They attacked the first Maltese fort, Saint Elmo, and their fire power was such that a Knight could not lift his head above the walls. Thirty who did so the first day, lost their lives. La Valette was hoping for ships and men from Sicily, so close it could be seen from Malta. The only ships that showed up were from North Africa, those of Suleiman. And the man chosen by Suleiman to lead them all was Mustapha, the young Turk present years before at Rhodes.

Roger Crowley, in his wonderful *Empires of the Sea*, describes the hour-by-hour defense of the forts, by Knights, Maltese and others whose courage defies imagination. The defense of Malta truly ranks with the courage and perseverance of those at Salamis, Marathon and the Thermopylae, bulwarks all against the barbarian hordes from the East, courageous barbarians, fanatical even, but mindless cannon fodder ruled by tyrants.

The first fort gave way, massacred to the last man, all 1,500. The heads of the leaders were raised on the top of the fort, at the end of lances; their disemboweled bodies were dressed in their knightly white and red and nailed to crosses. La Valette had the heads of all the captured Turks fired from cannons into Ottoman lines.

When news of the massacre reached Venice the Venetians danced in the streets, perhaps to gain the goodwill of Suleiman who would permit Venetian trade to resume. In fact, Suleiman used the Doge of Venice to pass on his messages to the pope and European kings, this being the fastest way to communicate. Throughout the entire Renaissance the Serenissima never ever reacted like the rest of Europe.

One "Ottoman," a Greek from the Peloponnesus, captured as a child and now an important janissary, swam to the Knights' position and divulged extremely important information concerning Mustapha's intentions. The man, now nearly 60, reconverted to Christianism. Philip II finally was able to infiltrate 700 reinforcements into Malta, an enormous boon but unbelievably little considering the thousands of eager volunteers waiting on Sicily to help the Knights. European indecision, then as today, was and is the Achilles' heel of these otherwise great peoples. Another Greek slave, this one held by the Knights, tried to warn the Turks of the reinforcements. He was caught and butchered.

Astonishingly, the Turks got 60 galleys into the blockaded harbor by bringing them overland along greased planks, pulled by oxen. These boats, aided by land forces, attacked the remaining forts. But the Knights had positioned a number of cannons in hidden locations and thanks to them the Muslim attack was not only halted, the Muslims eventually were forced to retreat, leaving 4,000 of their own floating in the harbor and spread out in front of the forts. Four Ottomans were captured and interrogated before being turned over to the Maltese to be literally torn apart. Due to the massacre of the first fort, no one would be spared from then on.

In Spain Philip had rebuilt the fleet, but now he hesitated to use it, so great was his fear of the Ottomans and the near certainty, in his mind, of the fleet being destroyed. The gene of decisiveness had simply not been transmitted from Charles V to his boy Philip II. Men of undaunted courage were dying on Malta, with other men and ships, on Sicily, in full view of the Maltese, chomping at the bit to help.

Suleiman sent a message, through the Doge of Venice, to Mustapha, ordering him to accomplish his task. And Mustapha, despite the loss of thousands of his crack troops, the janissaries, moved to do so. Mustapha and La Valette were equally experienced, equally skilled, equally inflexible, but not equally prepared. Muslim thoroughness was so complete that there were daily lists of valorous men and the recompense offered by the sultan to each.

The Ottomans buried their dead, sculpting out mass graves from the sold rock surface, the bodies of which huge numbers of Muslims lost their lives trying to retrieve. La Valette, desperately needing every man, forbade the retrieval of their own losses.

With winter on the horizon the rains came, bloating the bodies, bringing death, especially to the Ottomans, in the form of dysentery, the most disgusting form of misery, that emptied the body of its substance while poisoning the atmosphere, already filthy due to the rotting, stinking, unburied bodies.

The enemy was so close that at times they could exchange news. Janissaries captured as small boys could remember enough of their original Italian, Greek or Spanish to give vent to their misery to the Christians facing them, heartbreaking scenes between these men who could have been, for all they knew, brothers separated during infancy.

On Sicily 11,000 men waited word from Philip to cross the 30 miles between the two islands. In Turkey Suleiman awaited news of victory from Mustapha, the sultan's life measured now in just a few remaining months.

Then a miracle. A horseman was seen riding with terrible haste towards Mustapha's tent, whipping his horse mercilessly. The animal fell and the rider took his scimitar and struck off its legs in revenge. He ran to Mustapha's carpeted tent to tell him that Philip had finally awoken from his lethargy. The long-awaited reinforcements from Sicily were on the horizon. Mustapha, whom Suleiman later permitted to keep his head, gave orders to pack up.

The siege of Malta was at an end.

Six years later, on nearly the day of Caravaggio's birth, Marcantonio Colonna, Costanza's father (Costanza who would be a faithful friend throughout all of Caravaggio's life), led the forces that destroyed the Ottoman fleet for good, in a naval engagement known as the Battle of Lepanto.

– 2 –

Most sources believe that becoming a Knight had been a wish Caravaggio had often expressed, and it played in well with the extremes of his character, from a painter nearly as acclaimed as Michelangelo, to a killer on the run, to a monk in the service of Malta. He would renounce the princely life he had led with del Monte, eating and drinking and fucking the best that life had to offer, pushing his way through the alleys of Rome, dagger at easy reach, spending the wild sums his paintings now procured. He would exchange instant justice at the end of his sword in favor of vows of poverty, obedience and chastity. He, Michelangelo da Caravaggio, would trade the good life for the life of a saint. He had convinced himself that this was the right path, just as he and the people about him had convinced themselves throughout all their lives of the existence of good and bad, that a soul left purgatory the instant a coin hit a priest's alms bowl, and that absolution came through confession. Like sex, after the first act of faith one was no longer virgin.

The promise of a painting or two opened all the doors to knighthood for Caravaggio. But the Grand Master, Wignacourt, needed the consent of the pope himself, a pope who, for the moment, hesitated to absolve Caravaggio of the killing of Tomassoni, but who planned, too, to squeeze, like a lemon, the last *chef d'oeuvre* from the rustic artist. Wignacourt was intelligent, modest, always ready to accept advice, generous and, when he had the information he needed, decisive. He had rule over 1,800 monks

(Knights), half on Malta itself, and was ever ready to protect his subjects from the Moors who tried to capture and then sell them as slaves. He even set up a fund to ransom those captured before he took power. To say the least, he was lionized.

In Wignacourt's request to Pope Paul he didn't mention Caravaggio's name as the recipient of the knighthood, but he did mention that the man in question had been accused of murder, and as all of Italy had had little to gossip about other than Cenci's assassination and Ranuccio's killing, there was no doubt in the pope's mind as to the recipient's identity.

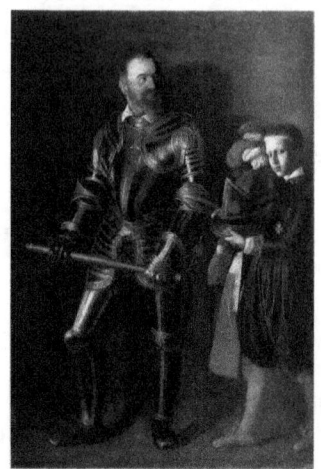

Wignacourt and one of his pages by Caravaggio.

While waiting for word from Paul which, unusual for him, would be sent back on the very next ship to Malta, Caravaggio did several portraits of Wignacourt, one of which showed him in the presence of one of his many pages. Every historian since that time has added two and two, making Wignacourt the king of pederasts, but naturally no one will ever know. The pages were lads chosen from the ranks of poor nobles, and it is said that Wignacourt paid for their education from is own pocket.

Caravaggio was meek in the presence of Wignacourt, whose unassertive manner nonetheless hid a fist of iron. Wignacourt was a military leader of extremely long experience, and not for a moment would a mere painter like Caravaggio pose the slightest problem. Whether Caravaggio just played at being meek in order to be accepted as a monk and to mollify the other Knights, aristocrats for whom Caravaggio and his plebeian blood counted for nothing, is unknown. But Caravaggio had arrived in Rome with literally not a scudo in his pocket; had allied himself with riff-raff like Longhi who adored assaulting merchants who showed him inadequate respect; had most probably set himself up as a part-time pimp; and had wounded several men, killing one--all of which meant that he had the potential of a streetwise hard-core killer, and no matter how much Wignacourt thought himself capable of controlling the situation, he may have let a wolf in among sheep.

Caravaggio had come to Malta on one of the red-and-gold Maltese ships captained by none other than Fabrizio Sforza Colonna, one of Constanza's sons, now Captain-General of the Knights of Malta's fleet! The boats were crowded--up to 500 men--and filthy, rowed by oarsmen in the absence of wind. The heat was intolerable, disease flourished, and the rowers were cadenced by drums and the blows of whips.

Wignacourt loved Malta and had been literally there to see the spectacular capital, Valletta, an immensely fortified town, rise from the island's cliffs and throne over the deep harbor. Although he died at age 71, before the city's completion, he wished to beautify it with churches and Caravaggio's art. Caravaggio came through with his most outstanding creation, the *Beheading of St. John the Baptist*, the only painting he signed with his name, *F Michelangelo*, the F for Fra' as he had succeeded in being made a monk. His signature was in blood--how seemingly typical of this man who had personally known and personally been responsible for so much suffering--blood from the throat of the saint, his head pressed solidly against the ground by his assassin, while the assassin's other hand hides the offending knife behind his back. He stares down at his victim, set on the sight of the gushing blood, hypnotized even, as if thinking, "*I, the living, have ended this life. I am God. I am misery. And the sight of your suffering has engorged my penis with the blood of the living, and I shall insert it into the living, and my orgasm will confirm my being alive!*" The assassin is a true Derek Jarman male, as found in his film *Sebastian*, virile to the extreme, his hair short--incredibly so for the times--his skin glistening. John the Baptist was the Knights' protector, then as he is today.

His name written in the blood gushing from the throat of John the Baptist, the only time Caravaggio signed a work, the horror of the slaughter has never been equaled in painting, sculpture or film, proof that no one then as today has risen to the convoluted complexity of the man known as Caravaggio. Pressed to the floor by his assassin, the horror is amplified by the virility of the man holding John down, his knife held at the ready behind his back to finish the decapitation. John, old, frail and helpless, draws our attention thanks to his bright red robe.

The Beheading of St. John the Baptist is one of the two greatest masterpieces executed by Caravaggio, the other being *David with the Head of Goliath*, both done in Malta, this one in 1608. As described elsewhere, Caravaggio, named a Knight of St. John, was soon to be defrocked, in absentia, by his peers, in the very room his *Beheading* would hang.

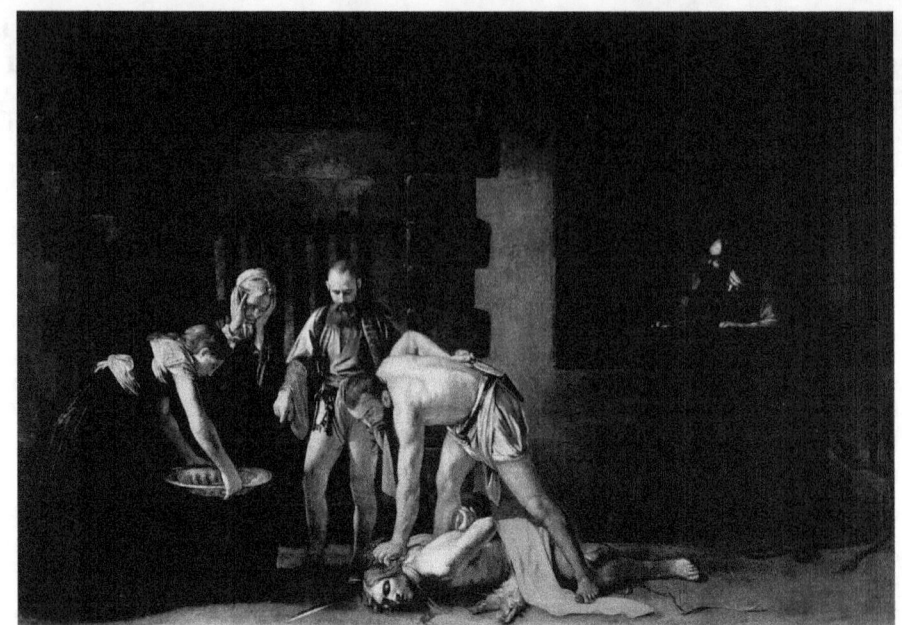

The Beheading of St. John the Baptist

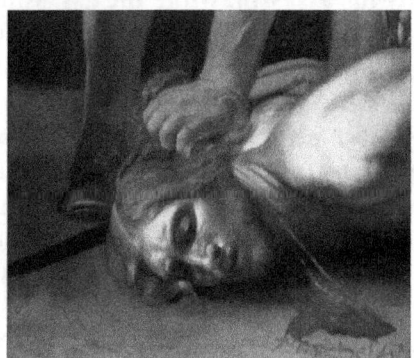

Detail

- 3 -

And then, when things were going perfectly, Caravaggio, in Malta, threw a wrench in the works. Everything had started off so well! He was adored by the Grand Master, adulated by the Knights, worshipped by the Maltese. True, he couldn't stride the streets armed to the teeth as he had in Rome, accompanied by his faithful dogs, like Onorio Langhi and Minniti, pushing citizens out of the way, eating and drinking without paying, and fucking alongside his buddies, when not fucking his buddies. He just had to wait it out, a few weeks longer, perhaps even just a few days, until a red-and-gold Maltese boat brought word from Paul that his hand was needed in

Rome to paint pictures, and that all was pardoned and forgiven. After all, who was Ranuccio Tomassoni, other than a boy who had wished to live out his life?

But he screwed up--the least that can be said. Again, not only are details lacking, but we don't even see the big picture. Some said he butt-fucked one of Wignacourt's pages--the Grand Master's own personal reserve (this according to some sources certain of Wignacourt preference for boys--but far from all sources). Others say he killed someone in a duel, this on an island where there were hundreds of testosterone-engorged men and boys, men who may have had the title of monk but were first and foremost men. Any pretext for a duel is conceivable, from making a pass at a man's whore to looking at a man, as I've written, a nanosecond too long. One major source believes that what he did so deeply offended Wignacourt that he set out to destroy the artist. Another source believes he offended an important personage (through an insult? by physically injuring him?) who got him locked in jail and, when he escaped, set the wheels in motion that finally led to his death at age 38. In this version not only was Wignacourt not against him, Wignacourt had done everything necessary to ensure his escape.

Then again, perhaps his problem had had a totally other origin. Perhaps he had been treated disrespectfully by one of the many sons of the Knights. Caravaggio was now a Knight himself, but he knew he would never be accepted as such by the island's nobles. And yet he was a dear friend of the Grand Master, Wignacourt. He was the pet of popes. His painting was hailed as the best in existence--new, awesomely naturalistic, and the wish of everyone with money and power was to possess one, from Wignacourt to Pope Paul, from Cardinal Scipione Borghese to the Colonna. How dare anyone stand in his way, and especially not these young Maltese pups, aristocracy flotsam compared to the man of talent that was Michelangelo Merisi da Caravaggio. In this case any one of a million slights might have made him reach for his sword and wound some young seigneur, landing him in prison. Caravaggio was the son of a palazzo steward, he was not noble and nobly born. He in no way earned his knighthood, felt many of the Knights and their knightly sons. Caravaggio would never admit the fact that he lacked nobility, but the truth haunted his innermost being. Just a word, just one, in some tavern by a drunken princeling, would have triggered the hatred in his heart that had metastasized through years of ass licking, beginning with those who had taken him in after the death of his father, to the workshops where he had cleaned the toilets and, most probably, been forced to accept what awaited him every night at the hands of the master and the bigger boys. Doffing his cap when del Monte took a drink, bending to the will of Pope Paul and the nobles because he somehow lacked the inner fire and determination of a Michelangelo Buonarroti to resist, nor did he have the immense intelligence of a da Vinci to guide him through the world's shark-filled waters. In blind rage he had struck out, because he in no way had the gifts of a Cyrano de Bergerac: to turn insult into rhetorical vengeance.

Graham-Dixon informs us that recent research indicates that Caravaggio and several others were involved in an attack on a friar, Giovanni Roero. Like Caravaggio, his fellow assailants had criminal backgrounds, not abnormal for a brotherhood based on militancy. Roero had been shot. Nothing more has come to light.

The prison he entered was Fort Sant'Angelo, his home for the coming weeks. His cell was chiseled from the rock in the form of a beehive, like the Mycenaean tomb of Agamemnon, eleven feet deep and capped with an iron grille. Prisoners were lowered and raised by rope. While Caravaggio languished behind bars, Wignacourt was unveiling his monumental (10 feet high by 15 feet long) *The Beheading of St. John* in a ceremony that alas fell flat due to the musicians, wanting more pay, who refused to play for the choir. The prison of Sant'Angelo was a place that was inescapable, unless accomplices had been given the necessary orders by Wignacourt. Or perhaps the head of the Maltese fleet, Constanza's son Fabrizio Sforza Colonna--who had brought Caravaggio to Malta--had decided on his own, or under orders from Wignacourt, to take him to Syracuse, the nearest port from Malta.

Interlude

The Musicians

Where I fail to see the signs of overt sexuality, as reviewers do in other of Caravaggio's paintings, in *The Musicians*--where most observers see misty-eyed boys celebrating love through the performance of madrigals--I see the main figure, Mario Minniti, in the throes of orgasm, his eyes glazed over, his mouth ecstatically ajar while emitting a sigh, his tongue sensually visible, his cheeks lustfully reddened.

The boys, three who are playing instruments, a fourth, an angel, reaching for grapes, were certainly added to the canvas separately, as some critics see a strong absence of cohesion. The end result is magisterial, especially considering that it was one of Caravaggio's very first works, painted while residing at the Palazzo Madama. The boys were certainly from del Monte's ''staff'', the fifty or so young men, artists, assistants and friends that del Monte used to tapestry his rooms, as the French say. The musical instruments, extremely expensive, obviously came from del Monte's personal collection, of which he was proud. The boy behind Minniti is probably Caravaggio himself, the head very similar to that in *The*

Boy Bitten by a Lizard.

The Musicians was lost for centuries until an antique dealer, in the 1930's, saw what he described as an interesting canvas. He bought it and then sold it to a captain for 100 pounds. A photo of the painting wound up in London where someone from the Metropolitan Museum saw it and paid $50,000, in 1952. X-rays show that the boy reaching for grapes had, originally, a quiver and wings. At one time the canvas was glued to a wooden support; this, and its being badly cared for, account for its poor state, say experts who have seen it up close.

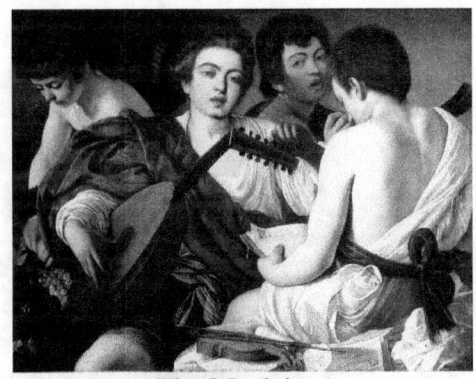

The Musicians

CHAPTER SIX

OTHER WORLDLY EVENTS

– 1 –

In keeping with my wish to provide a serious background to these events, let's bring things up to date: Elsewhere we have discussed and we will discuss Maximilian and his son Philip II, Charles V and *his* son Philip, François I and others. Here we'll continue to concentrate on the political aspects of Henry VIII, his son and daughters, as well as James I/VI, all of whom helped carry forth, in one way or another, the Renaissance.

Henry VIII's life is too well known to be belabored here. He had known and had interworked with all the giants of the times: Julius II who refused his divorce from his first wife Catherine; the Medici Leo X whose wish for peace with France inspired Henry to sign a treaty with Louis XII; Louis' son François I who met with Henry near Calais on what was dubbed the Cloth of Gold, two weeks of orgiastic all-out drinking and fucking French girls, ending in a wrestling match, proof that François had big muscles to go with his virility.

François, who had already lost his virginity to his sister at age 10, was a lad 6 ½ feet tall and so big some girls couldn't accommodate him although most tried, and, it was said, virgins literally lined up around his bed awaiting their chance to be deflowered--his specialty. His bed, as I've mentioned but can't help repeating, even accompanied him while he was out hunting, using it between kills, to the utter amazement of Henry VIII who had accompanied the king during his visit to France (Henry went far in such things, very far even, but not *that* far). François took whomever he wanted from the nobility, whether the ladies liked it or not, and apparently not all did as one woman had her husband infect himself with syphilis before infecting her so that she could infect the king. Another woman had her face slashed, which didn't dissuade François as it wasn't her face that interested him.

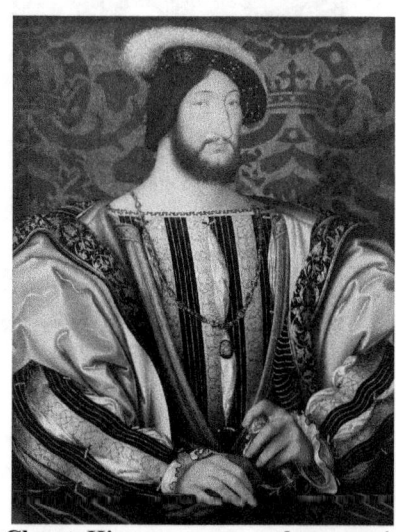

François I by Jean Clouet. His nose was greatly appreciated by demoiselles.

The day came for Cellini to present the finished statue to the king and his mistress. ''The Jupiter was raising his thunderbolt with the right hand in the act of hurling it; his left hand held the globe of the world. ''Among the flames of the thunderbolt I had very cleverly introduced a torch of white wax.'' Cellini had the king observe the statue from several angles, informing him that a sculpture should always be viewed from at least eight different standpoints. Cellini had draped some tissue around the statue's private parts, knowing a woman would be present, but when d'Étampes saw the statue she suggested to the king that the tissue was there to hid some imperfection. Cellini had Ascanio take it away. Madame d'Étampes stared at the incredible detail of the pubic bush, balls, penis and ample foreskin, and Cellini asked, ''Do you find it all as it should be?'' Madame d'Étampes left the room in a huff. As soon as she was gone the king ''exploded with laughter,'' says Cellini. (An extract from my book Cellini.)

Henry conspired with Charles V against the same François and was furious when the huge-jawed Spanish king freed François from Spanish captivity. Henry dilapidated the fortune left to him by his father Henry VII (who had taken the life of Perkin). He caused immeasurable suffering to his people, to his loyal servants, and the women he had lusted for, prior to murdering them.

From all sources his son Edward comes through as a delightful lad, made king at age 9, dead at age 16, two years before his majority. The years of his regency consisted of a series of rivalries without real interest here (or elsewhere for that matter). He was England's first born-and-bred Protestant monarch. He was universally described as kind and generous, and a scholar far beyond the lads of the other nobles. Henry VIII recognized his son for the jewel he was, raising him in hygienic conditions (the plague ever near), among the best minds in England. He sought to betroth the boy to seven-month-old Mary Queen of Scots, to which the Scots agreed before changing their minds, infuriating Henry to such a degree that he ordered massacres throughout Scotland, a horrible campaign known as The Rough Wooing. Henry died in horrible pain, small retribution for the thousands he had put to death while imposing the Anglican Church on England, which allowed him to fuck and murder whomever he wished.

Knowing he would soon die, young Edward worked hard to find a male to succeed him as king, but finding none, and deploring the "lack of issue from my body," he chose Lady Jane Grey. She would prove an unpopular choice and an army in Mary's favor would end her attempt to be crowned. Edward passed away, alas, in great pain, probably from tuberculosis, whispering at the end, "I am glad to die." His loss was terrible because like the youths the world over, he may have had the potential of a second Pericles.

Mary and Elizabeth were left behind. At age 37, the Catholic Mary, whose mother Catherine had been Spanish, decided it was time to marry a Catholic boy and bring forth a Catholic son who would bar the route to Protestant Elizabeth, her half-sister. She chose Prince Philip, Charles V's boy, which would bring England a good part of Europe, as well as the wealth of the New World (it was also this Philip who, through indecision, held back troops to fight against Suleiman on Malta). An act of parliament nonetheless made it clear that should Mary die, Philip would no longer be King of England. The marriage was unpopular because for patriotic reasons the people wanted her to marry an English lad, and also England--made Protestant thanks to Henry VIII's wish to rid himself of his wife Catherine--simply didn't appreciate two Catholics on the throne at the same time. Mary became pregnant to the surprise of Philip who found her too repulsive to "honor", as the French put it, and Elizabeth was freed from house arrest to witness the birth that would deprive her of the throne. Mary became huge, the time of her delivery came and then passed, finally ending, as one chronicler put it, "in a gigantic fart". Mary's failure to produce an heir was blamed by her co-religionists on her having tolerated Protestant heresy (symbolized by her refusal to put Protestant Elizabeth to death), thereby incurring God's wrath.

Along with her husband Philip, Mary entered into talks with Pope Julius III to reinstate Catholicism, after which Protestant nobles were put to death under heresy laws--although 800 had by then fled. The Archbishop of Canterbury, imprisoned, was forced to watch his priests burned at the stake. The archbishop renounced his Protestantism but was nonetheless set afire, renouncing his renouncement as the flames enveloped him.

When Charles V abdicated, Philip became King of Spain. Mary lost Calais to the French, reducing her prestige, and due to a prolonged wet season Englishmen began dying of famine. She herself died at age 42, perhaps of ovarian cancer, in pain like her father, and like her father responsible for countless horrible deaths.

Elisabeth was a religious pragmatist, deciding not to decide, an indecisiveness that marked her reign. The heresy laws were repealed and those who sought government employment simply had to swear allegiance to their new queen.

She had been in love and had slept with Robert Dudley since her adolescence, and he is thought to have killed his wife by pushing her down the stairs in order for Elizabeth and him to marry. They nonetheless remained close for 30 years. Her last of many suitors was the Duke d'Anjou, a bisexual cross-dresser 22 years her junior (10).

Concerning foreign policy, Elizabeth was concerned that Mary Queen of Scots, who had been raised in France, would prove the Trojan Horse by which the French would seize Scotland and then threaten England. Mary, for her part, was having her own problems. A Catholic in a Protestant country, she married the pretty Lord Darnley who killed her Italian secretary David Rizzio, believed to be *both* Darnley *and* Mary's lover.

Darnley, restrained by what he felt was Mary's obstinacy in recognizing him as co-king of Scotland, had ceased dining with her. The night of the murder, while she was enjoying a tête-à-tête with Rizzio during an intimate meal, Darnley was busy admitting the conspirators into Mary's palace. He entered the room through a secret passage behind a tapestry. He told Mary to not be too surprised, as a husband had the right to visit his wife. But he was immediately followed by men who demanded that she render Rizzio. Rizzio rose and stepped back into a window alcove. Instinctively Mary went to him, protecting him with her body, unaware that it was she the real target. Darnley tried to pull her aside while one of the conspirators lunged forward with a dagger, so close that Mary later said she felt the blade. Rizzio was wounded in the throat and fell to his knees, holding on to Mary's skirt, all the while begging for his life. Later still James, the son in her womb, her pregnancy so advanced that she was said to have been pregnant up to her neck, asserted that he had been told by those there that one man tried to run a sword into Mary's extended stomach, a sword another man purposefully deflected. Another put a pistol up to her side but, swore Mary later, it refused to discharge. Why Mary wasn't nonetheless dispatched is unknown. The men perhaps took pity on her condition. Darnley pulled her towards him, perhaps feeling that she had now been frightened enough to accord him his due without having to answer for her murder. After all, at the time Mary was still highly popular among the people. Rizzio was dragged down the winding stairs behind the tapestry where a score of men awaited with drawn daggers. Still pleading, he was literally cut to ribbons by those who had witnessed months of his mincing gate, fine apparel and gifted speech. Thrown into an unmarked grave, he left History for eternity. (An extract from my book *Christ has his John, I have my George, The History of British Homosexuality*.)

Darnley was blown up in his home (his body was found outside where the explosion supposedly threw it, but as he was still alive he was throttled to death). His murderer was purportedly the Earl of Bothwell whom Mary then married. Due to all of this, and due to her Catholicism, she was forced to abdicated in favor of her and Darnley's son James. She bolted to England where she was imprisoned for 19 years before being tried for attempting to overthrow Elizabeth, earning her decapitation.

Elizabeth was excommunicated but kept her head by decreeing that only priests who came to England with the mission of converting the English to Catholicism would lose theirs. Many did.

She knighted Sir Francis Drake for his circumnavigation of the globe from 1577 to 1580, opening an era of English piracy thanks to English naval superiority. As Spain was the chief target for attacks, King Philip II (former King of England) sent an enormous and extremely costly armada against Elizabeth, one that was destroyed due to a serious of uncanny events, like a sudden horrific storm.

Elizabeth sent troops to France to help Protestant Henry IV gain the French throne but then Henry, ever pragmatic, converted to Catholicism, stating that "Paris was well worth a mass." He was beloved by his people, one of whom nevertheless stabbed him in the heart (10).

Elizabeth sent troops to Catholic Ireland to prevent a landing zone for Catholic Spain. The Irish, considered barbarians, were slaughtered, down to women and children, and their lands scorched so they would die of hunger. In Muster alone 30,000 starved to death.

Wars and poor harvests impoverished the English, and the only bright light was the genius of Shakespeare and Marlow (11), the advent of whom had nothing whatsoever to do with the Virgin Queen.

She favored young men until the end. How many had access to her rich bed and moldy body will never be known.

James, Elizabeth's successor, was a true Renaissance man in that he went from men to women in total abandon, *à la Florentine*, as had Lorenzo

Il Magnifico, a connoisseur of every form of love/lust. During the restoration of Apethorpe Hall in 2004-2008 a secret passage was found that had linked James' bedroom to that of his then favorite, George Villiers, Duke of Buckingham (13). His contemporaries remarked that his predecessor, Elizabeth, a known flirt who didn't fear war, was King, while James, who insisted on peace, was Queen (*Rex fuit Elizabeth, nunc est regina Jacobus*). He was nonetheless happily married to Anne of Denmark who gave him *seven* children while suffering through two stillbirths and three miscarriages.

As mentioned but bears repeating: his mother was Mary, Queen of Scots, beheaded by Elizabeth for plotting Elizabeth's death. Mary had been forced to abdicate by Scottish Protestants and had fled to England in hopes of Elizabeth's aid. James was crowned King of Scotland at age 13 months. His father Lord Darley had been blown up in his home, perhaps because he had ordered the death of his wife's suspected lover, David Rizzio, which took place in front of Mary while she was trying to protect Rizzio who was literally seeking shelter in her skirts. Rizzio, young and handsome, was also the purported lover of Darley himself, equally young and handsome.

Thus began a line of regents to stand in for the thirteen-month-old King of Scotland, beginning with Mary's half-brother James Steward, assassinated by James Hamilton. Mathew Stewart became the baby's second regent, killed in battle against Mary's supporters. The third regent, the Earl of Mar, was poisoned by James Douglas, 4th Earl of Morton. Morton was executed, not for Mar's poisoning but for his role in James' father Darley's murder.

James was then 15 and placed himself under a series of favorites, beginning with a handsome Frenchman, Esmé Stewart, Sieur d'Aubigny, the future Earl of Lennox, later made the only duke of Scotland. He was forced to leave due to his introducing the boy ''to carnal lust,'' and the boy hadn't as yet enough power to prevent it. But soon he did and Lennox was replaced by Robert Carr, Earl of Somerset, followed by George Villiers, Duke of Buckingham, and many other lovers, handsome pages as well as young nobles. During this period the peoples of Scotland and England congratulated the king on his chastity, as he showed no interest in women. James, like boys the world over, took his pleasure when and where and how he wished, seen or unseen, known or unknown, and, thankfully, this is the way it will always be.

James became King of England in 1603 upon the death of the last Tudor, Elizabeth. The transition was made smooth thanks to secret negotiations between James and Elizabeth's chief minister, Sir Robert Cecil, and just hours after Elizabeth expired James was declared king. He was welcome with open arms in London by a people thankful that the succession had been peaceful. As prearranged, Cecil and Elizabeth's counselors remained in place, until James had the reins of government securely in hand.

James was interested in witchcraft, which led to the writing of his book *Daemonologie*. He was convinced that witches had sent storms in order to kill him while at sea and personally arranged the torture and burning of several. On the eve of the opening of parliament, which he would preside over accompanied by the queen and his children, Guy Fawkes was discovered in the cellars arranging a pile of wood next to 36 barrels of gunpowder. Fawkes and other conspirators were executed, and the day, known as Guy Fawkes Day (or Night), is celebrated even now with fireworks. He executed Walter Raleigh, one of Elizabeth's lovers, when he came back from an expedition seeking gold in South America, the reason being that Raleigh had exchanged fire with the Spanish there, something James had absolutely forbidden due to his policy of keeping the peace with Spain, and his wish to marry his son to the Spanish king's daughter, the Infanta. This greatly disturbed the people because Raleigh was held in great esteem and because no one wanted the English to kowtow to the Spanish. James was in no hurry to marry his son off, because even if the marriage took years to conclude, during that time there would be no war with Spain.

But before the marriage took place he had a stroke and died, afflicted by arthritis and gout.

His son Charles was unpopular in England because of his taxation and his choice of a Catholic wife, and unpopular in Scotland because he tried to impose his Protestant beliefs on the Catholic population. Both peoples rose up against him. He was executed and the monarchy was abolished. The Church of England was put aside in favor of Puritanism, established to reform it. England became a Republic with Cromwell, a puritan, at its head. The House of Lords was abolished because its members were there through hereditary, not meritocracy. Then in 1660 the monarchy under Charles's son was reestablished, along with the House of Lords. The Church of England was reinstated. The people of England went back to the comfort of their former yoke, happily subservient to church, royalty and lords to this very day.

As we have seen, the powers preceding the death of *Il Magnifico* were the Medici, popes Alexander VI and Julius II, the French kings Charles VIII, Louis XII and François I, the Sforza for a limited time, Cesare Borgia, the condottiere Montefeltro, the cities of Florence, Milan and Rome, as well as a scattering of city-states such as Ferrara and Venice. The Serenissima had an uncanny way of butting out of other peoples' affairs when there was potential danger, but didn't hesitate to send troops when victory and gain seemed certain.

Then a score of years following the death of *Il Magnifico* Charles V came on the scene, bringing order out of chaos following the massacre of thousands and the destruction of Rome. He brought Pope Clement VII to heel by kissing the pope's ring, and the pope, behind the scenes, kissed Charles' ass, even coronating him emperor, the last pope to ever do so. And what a royal ass! At age 16 he was crowned Charles I, King of a Spanish Empire that included Naples, Sardinia, Sicily, Navarre, parts of Asia and the New World. At 19, as Charles V, he ruled, as emperor, over Europe. And then, age 54, he gave it all up, making his brother Holy Roman Emperor and his son King of Spain. Two years afterwards, in a monastery, at peace with himself or not, he offered up his soul to God, a soul responsible for hundreds of thousands of deaths in Europe, and millions in the New World and Asia, owing to Pizarro, Cortés and Magellan, and Spanish invincibility--courageous, professional and utterly determined men who overcame such odds that the scope of their conquests remains incomprehensible to this very day--as well as a consequence of diseases, especially smallpox, that the conquistadors harbored on their persons. The answer as to why the Spanish sailed to the New World was perfect encapsulated by the conquistador Bernal del Castillo: "We went to serve God and his Majesty, to give light to those in darkness and to acquire the wealth men covet."

Charles was an important mover in attempts to reduce friction between Catholics and Protestants. He did this through the Council of Trent, a council that took place in Trento Italy. Protestantism was denounced but it was decided that the way to combat it was through peaceful and intellectual means. A standard bible was commissioned and abuses, such as the sale of indulgences, were forbidden. There were 25 sessions, held under popes Paul II, Julius III and Pius IV. The next council wasn't held until 300 years afterwards. This and other moves of Charles earned him the reputation as a man "greedy of peace and quiet."

Charles' most famous quote was: "I speak Spanish to God, Italian to women, French to men and German to my horse."

The problems that arose between Charles, Henry VIII, François I and a number of popes began with the election of Charles as Holy Roman Empire, a prestigious position desired by Henry VIII and François I. Reign over the Holy Roman Empire was an elective monarchy and the electors, around seven in number, came from princes who chose the emperor in Germany before having him crowned by the pope. Besides losing the election to Charles, Henry VIII earned Charles' wrath when he tried to divorce Charles' aunt, Catherine. On the other hand Charles was a natural ally of Pope Leo X because they both wished to put an end to Protestantism and its founder, Martin Luther. As usual, Venice was in the background, seeking a way to gain profit by allying itself with whichever side held promise of being victorious. War broke out between Charles and François I when the French attempted to recuperate disputed Navarre. Henry VIII, Pope Leo X and Charles formed an alliance, the result of which led to François' defeat at Pavia, the decimation of French nobility, and the capture of François himself--all on Charles' 25th birthday.

Shortly after Charles' death his son Philip was named the new King of Spain, Naples, Sicily and Sardinia, Duke of Milan, as well as King of England and Ireland during his marriage to Queen Mary I. He ruled in the New World and the Philippines were named after him. It was during Philip's reign that the expression was coined, "The Empire on which the sun never sets," later adopted by the English. Philip was born and raised in Spain and cared little for Germans who cared little for him. An ardent Catholic, he raised havoc in the Netherlands by trying to destroy their deep-seated Protestantism, whereas his father, Charles, had not been overly harsh with Protestants, and had thusly kept the peace throughout his kingdom. Philip was described as physically attractive--although his chin, too, was immense--tastefully dressed, courteous and gracious. His father had supposedly taught him to be modest, patient and to distrust everyone. He was said to have had "a smile that cut like a sword" and icy self-control.

Events went Philip's way too in Portugal where the king died without descendants, only to be succeeded by an uncle who died too without heirs. Havoc irrupted when three grandchildren fought for the throne but influential members of the Portuguese government, wanting stability, escaped to Spain where they threw their weight behind Philip who became Philip I of Portugal. He robbed the Portuguese treasury but allowed the country to keep its laws, currency and own government, run in concert with a council on Portugal that Philip set up in Madrid.

One of Charles V's masterstrokes was marrying Philip to the Queen of England, age 37, to Philip's 27. Once the marriage was consummated and the blood-strained sheets viewed by all, the English did what they could to ensure that power was shared equally between the two monarchs, down to the coins that represented them both holding the same crown. The marriage contract contained but one major codicil, that England would not be obliged to follow Charles in his spendthrift wars. There would be no bankruptcy in England. Documents were translated into Latin or Spanish so they could be read by the foreign king. Mary died too soon to reestablish the Catholic church in England, and with her death Philip lost the totality of his powers and influence. When Elizabeth became queen, Philip proposed marriage but was refused.

Philip nonetheless tried to maintain peace between his maternal country and his adopted country, even throwing his support to Elizabeth when the pope threatened her with excommunication. But Elizabeth's discriminatory policies against Catholics in England, her support of Protestants outside England, notably in the Netherlands, and her support of English piracy against the Spanish--a source of wealth for England as well as an ardent virility for her bed in the form of Walter Raleigh--obliged Philip, the jilted lover, to turn offensive.

The catalyst was the execution of Mary Queen of Scots, Philip's last hope of seeing a Catholic leader--as Mary I and he himself had been--at the head of the English Empire. He sent a fleet to invade the country where he had been king, with the hope of bringing an end to Protestantism. The fleet was destroyed by storms, as mentioned, and by English naval mastery. Undaunted, he sent three more fleets over the following ten years, none of which came to anything. War ended only with Elizabeth and his deaths. He was the first sovereign to personally see to his sailors' medical care, providing pensions to those who survived and compensation to the families of those killed in battle. His own death was atrocious, following a combination of factors that left him so bedridden that a hole had to be cut in his mattress to evacuate his body fluids.

Philip was followed by his son Philip III whose older brother died insane. (Hapsburg inbreeding would eventually destroy the lot.) Adjectives describing him are: undistinguished, insignificant, weak, dim-witted, *et j'en passe.* One said his only virtue appeared to reside in a total absence of vice, another that he cared only for hunting and travel. He ruled the Spanish Empire through the Duke of Lerma who filtered those who could see the king; in this way Lerma accumulated immeasurable wealth. Lerma also amassed art treasures, most of which were personal gifts to him or, through him, to Philip III, and are found today in the Prado. He expulsed the Moriscos from Spain, Moors who had nonetheless converted to Catholicism but who remained apart in appearance, customs and some rites inherited from Islam. The expulsions impoverished the country as they deprived Spain of cheap labor. From then on agriculture failed and famines took countless lives, as did the plague. The Moors, around 300,000, were shipped to Tunis and Morocco, under the escort of 30,000 soldiers. Children under age seven were forbidden to leave, however, in order to protect them from being converted to Islam. In addition, Philip saw to it that a law was passed forbidding their being sold as slaves. Spain was impoverished by the loss of the Moors, but not the rich who took over their lands. Yet the loss was less than that when the Jews were expulsed in 1492. Lerma was eventually deposed by his son, but the pope named him a cardinal, one who outlived the king who stood passively by while Lerma's son took the reins of power. His son tried to despoil the father, but Lerma had put aside so much wealth that the boy was able to dissipate only a smidgen.

A final break to bring in the story of the Renaissance Wars, vital in the history of Italy at the time, but included here exclusively to round off the historical events that took place preceding and during Caravaggio's lifetime. This part does not add to the life or the works of Caravaggio, and so the reader can safely skip it, should he/she wish to do so, and go directly to the next chapter.

In the first part I exposed the peoples and events that made the Renaissance intellectually and humanistically possible. Some men collected and translated our Greek heritage while others fought over kingdoms as they did table scraps. The nobles led the way into battles, followed by the likes of the Swiss, the Gascons, the landsknechts, who would dash a child's head against a wall and spread a nun's legs until it leaked the colors of the Knights of St. John, red and white, blood and semen, especially if the rapists of nuns were Lutheran. Juan Borgia strutted through the streets of Rome, gorgeous in his velvet black trousers and doublet, his shirt a splendid white, his hand gently caressing the codpieces that accentuated his loins, an invitation to any handsome lass or lad. And so it was and will ever be: the intelligence that sent us to the moon will always be surpassed by the reptilian segment of the brain, and blood and sperm, in ever and ever and ever greater quantities will spill into--and fertilize--the nourishing earth.

The genesis of the Renaissance Wars began well before 1494 but here we'll take them up after the death of Alexander VI and that of Juan Borgia's brother, Cesare. We'll start our story with the League of Cambrai.

The expansion of Venice over the centuries had made enemies, and as Venice, like a spoiled child, always decided what was best for itself, a city-state either won against Venice or lost and gave in: there was no intermediary negotiation. The Venetians didn't hesitate a second in aligning themselves with the Ottomans when they felt their commerce--a lifeline without which they would cease to exist--was threatened. After all, one of their most vital possessions, Cyprus, was in spitting distance from Turkey. At the same time, Venice always found a reason not to come to the aid of the pope or an invading force from France or Spain, unless it could reap easy benefits.

The Venetians had thusly made enemies. Strangely, it was in the surrounding territories they ruled that the rural classes, the farmers, supported them because the Venetians were vultures of a far less aggressive nature than the nobles in places like Padua, Verona and Vicenza whom the farmers' found far more arrogant and who, especially, taxed them to death.

As all the great powers had lost something to the Serenissima, they met to form the League of Cambrai to get everything back: Louis XII,

Maximilian, the city-states of Mantua and Ferrara, and Pope Julius II who wanted to recapture the totality of the Papal States.

When the Venetians learned of the League of Cambrai and knew for certain that an invasion was eminent, they closed ranks and raised the money needed for an army.

The French were the first to "enter the dance," as the French themselves put it, with the battle of Agnadello. They came with their own men but they also wanted to complete their forces with the Swiss. While the cantons met to decide whether or not to participate, the French went over their heads, directly to the Swiss mercenaries themselves. They thought that all they needed was adequate bribes, and bribes did secure them several thousand mercenaries who needed the money, but not the expert forces provided by the cantons who, tired of being treated like bumpkins by the arrogant French, refused to participate. The Swiss, like the Venetians, would always march to a different drummer, then as today.

The Venetians were drubbed at Agnadello, especially as they refused to commit their entire forces, saving a large number to protect their island kingdom, where they now withdrew. With incredible intelligence, they advised towns like Verona, Padua and Vicenza to surrender to the Holy Roman Emperor Maximilian, knowing that they would be able to win these places back, later, far more easily than if they surrendered to the French.

So the Venetians found themselves back home, but with their military largely intact, while all around them the farmers, who preferred them to the nobles who had now resumed power over them, began guerilla tactics against the invaders, the French and the troops of Maximilian, who were just beginning to arrive.

The Venetian genius continued when the Serenissima unilaterally gave back every position they had appropriated, including everything Julius wanted. They did the same with their Spanish positions, the Venetian ports surrounding Naples, and they didn't even wait for Ferdinand to contact them, they sent embassies to *him* revealing their decision. They tried to do the same with Maximilian but failed. Both Pope Julius and Ferdinand of Spain decided that a vital, living Venice would serve them better against the unbeatable French, and so they united their forces to reduce the power of Louis XII. That left only Maximilian as a major player in Louis' corner. Deeply religious, Maximilian would not fight against the pope, and when Ferdinand assured Maximilian that Maximilian's own son, Charles, would rule over Spain on the 20th birthday, Maximilian returned to the comforts of Vienna. Venice then took back Padua and Vicenza as they had foreseen, leaving only Verona in the hands of Louis. The pope got the Swiss cantons to provide him with 6,000 men, the best fighting force in Europe, men he paid extremely well, men he put aside as a spearhead should one be needed.

Then a *coup de théâtre*: Julius, afraid of Louis XII's growing power, proved himself to be the warrior pope History would crown him as being by forming the Holy League, Holy because it was he at its head. Amazingly, incredibly, it would consist of Venice. Julius, who just basically wanted the Venetians to remain neutral, only asked the Serenissima to give the League the soldiers they wished to volunteer. Ferdinand of Spain would provide most of the troops and even Henry VIII was invited, Ferdinand promising him his aid in Aquitaine (a huge chunk of France vital to the English as you may remember from the story of Henry II and Eleanor, so brilliantly played out in *A Lion in Winter*). It was announced that the League was absolutely not aimed at Louis, although it was.

The next year's campaign, that of 1511, in the absence of Louis who remained in France, was marked by Louis' men's attack on Brescia and the horrible sack of the town that was to follow. The attack took place in torrential rain and the French sustained many casualties. French infantry consisted mostly of Gascons and landsknechts, the dregs of humanity, who massacred and raped over a period of five days. 4,000 cartloads of stolen goods left the burning town, the soldiers now so rich that many simply returned home to France. The result was satisfying in the sense that the next town, Bergamo, paid the French 60,000 ducats to escape from the same fate.

The next battle saw Spanish and papal forces against the French at Ravenna, said to have been the costliest massacre in troops in centuries. Perhaps 20,000 men and boys lost their lives, with a French win thanks to French cavalry, but with the loss of the cream of the French nobility. Cardinal Giovanni de' Medici, the future Leo X, was taken prisoner. But the French had been weakened and Julius and his Swiss mercenaries, aided by the Venetians, chased Louis' troops from Milan where they installed Massimiliano Sforza. Louis' troops went back to France. It was 1511. 48 years of wars still remained.

What followed was more Byzantine than the convoluted Byzantines themselves. Take, for example, just the case of Verona. Louis XII died, a great king who was said to have died in supposed bliss while ''honoring'' his new bride, Henry VIII's sister, perhaps a bit young and demanding for the old man. His son François I took the throne (a king amply covered elsewhere) and retook Milan, showing his acumen by bringing Milan's new ruler, Massimiliano, to France where he was offered a wife and 30,000 ducats. François then wanted to take Verona from Maximilian who requested that François--having far stronger forces than those of Maximilian--not humiliate him by allowing him to hand Verona over to the Venetians who had now sided with the French. A treaty was drawn up giving Verona to Maximilian's son Charles who immediately gave it to the

French who immediately handed it over to their new ally the Venetians. From here on Venice more or less leaves the scene as the Serenissima had suffered more than in its entire history. During the wars the Venetian town of Vicenza, for example, had changed hands 36 times, bringing massacre to the people with each upheaval, death, famine and rape, a worse fate than Hell itself.

Ferdinand now died, leaving the Spanish throne to Maximilian's son Charles, age 15. Four years later Maximilian himself died and Charles, thanks to his pugnacity and intelligence, became the most important person of his times, King of Spain, Naples and Sicily, and Holy Roman Emperor.

Julius died, replaced by the Medici Leo X who brought Florence back into the Medici lap. The Spanish troops who helped bring this about sacked Prato first, a town that had been sold to Florence in 1351 by Naples, a landmark massacre during which 6,000 were killed, a massacre remembered by Pratoans to this very day, summed up in a letter by an Italian to a friend, ''Oh God, oh God, oh God, what cruelty!'' The Florentines paid the Spanish 80,000 ducats to escape the same fate, with an additional 20,000 to the Spanish general.

The year was 1519 and there were still 40 years of inhuman suffering before the end of the Renaissance Wars.

In 1520 François decided to destabilize the very young Charles by backing revolts among the Länder in Germany and dissident followers of Martin Luther. Charles, very religious, united with Pope Leo X to rid Italy of the French by naming Massimiliano's brother, Francesco Sforza, Duke of Milan. Leo felt that Charles would be the best bulwark against Luther, and confirmed his hold over Naples. As the Swiss cantons were split over aid to François and to Leo, both king and pope received several thousand mercenaries. Venice was obliged by treaty to aid François, and sent troops, but under anonymity.

Because the French had never been welcome rulers of Milan, and because the Venetians took the first opportunity to flee the city, the fall of Milan was immediate. But then Leo X died and papal funding of the war evaporated, bringing havoc as every city-state used the vacuum of power to free itself from any foreign presence.

Order came when Charles proved himself intellectually and militarily invincible. He would be a great king, but in his wake thousands of men and boys, women and children, would have their lives snuffed out. Then François, incapable of leaving well enough alone, invaded Italy. He was captured by Charles at Pavia and shipped to Spain.

The Treaty of Madrid gained François his freedom, but as he never envisaged respecting it, we won't go into its clauses except to say that the king was replaced by his two sons, both traumatized for life by the ordeal of their imprisonment.

Another League was formed, this one the League of Cognac, comprised of the new pope, another Medici, Clement VII, François I, Henry VIII, Florence and Francesco of Milan. Charles was invited, but as the intent of the League was to insure Italian independence of all foreign powers, he couldn't very well join. The aim, for Clement, was to place Naples--in the hands of Charles--under papal direction. François had joined the League as a bargaining chip to play in his hand with Henry and his hand with Charles. For Henry, the League was nothing but papal wind, but as he needed Clement to give him a divorce from Catherine of Aragon, Charles' aunt, he went along.

Then, on all sides, things began to go horribly wrong. Charles' troops, a huge percentage of which were mercenaries, were unpaid and reduced to scavenging for food. The papal forces disbanded because neither Henry nor François believed in the viability of the League, and Venice, as usual, withdrew it men in order to save them should Venice itself be attacked. Florentines, again unhappy under Medici rule, held back funds. With disorder everywhere, Charles' troops took things in hand by moving to Rome that they sacked. The doors of the city were closed to Charles' troops but his seasoned warriors had no trouble scaling the walls, slaughtering any man, woman or child that came in reach. As many, if not most, of the landsknechts were Lutheran, churches were especially designated targets in which the usual filth was etched on the frescoes, a playful landsknecht pope was elected and nuns repeatedly raped on the altars, good sport for these husky lads deprived of warmth, food, pillage and sex during the seemingly never-ending winter.

Naturally Charles was responsible. His lack of authority and failure to pay the troops on time led to his total loss of control over them. The sack went on for *eight months*, until there was literally nothing more to steal. To Charles' wretched troops were added thousands more, any peasant from the surrounding countryside who wanted in on the spoils. 12,000 people were killed and the population of Rome, due to the murders and those who fled the town, fell from 55,000 to 10,000 after the sack. Nearly all of the pope's Swiss guard was slain, an event commemorated to this day by the Michelangelo-clad boys who have descended from them.

Charles reestablished control and made a treaty with Clement VII. His troops left Rome and the pope left Castel Sant'Angelo where he had taken cover. He would later crown Charles Holy Roman Emperor in Bologna, at age 30, the last pope to do so. Facing religious unrest at home, Charles made peace with François. The Medici pope Clement VII had Charles promise to restore Medici rule over Florence by marrying his daughter to the Florentine Alessandro de' Medici. Francesco Sforza would remain

Duke of Milan and Clement recognized Charles' right to Naples. Venice got back some land and Ferrara lost some. François' sons were freed from Spain. Peace broke out following the Treaty of Barcelona signed in 1529. But 30 more years of havoc remained.

Charles tried to get Italian states to join him in still another league, the purpose of which was the members' protection in exchange for yearly financial backing. In this Charles was the original mafia boss offering security in exchange for ransom. But there was a secondary purpose: to show to François that Charles had plenty of friends, and so France would do well to watch its step.

Boredom nonetheless seeped through and François decided on still another Italian incursion. Like the English who nursed the chimera of kingship over France, so François convinced himself of French sovereignty over places like the Savoy, Nice, Genoa and Milan. As did the Venetians, he cast his net wide, opening negotiations with even Suleiman the Magnificent. He gave his son Henry II to Catherine de' Medici, giving him rights, François believed, to de' Medici Florence. (François had his mistress, Madame d'Étampes; his son Henry would have his mistress, Diane de Poitier; and Henry's wife Catherine would eventually evolve into one of the most extraordinary personages in history [10].)

Francesco died in Milan of natural causes and Charles took over the city-state, the perfect justification for François' renewed intervention.

Paul III became pope and welcomed Charles into Rome with full honors, as Charles was now the most powerful prince in the world and the pope could benefit from his reflected glory. Paul initiated a meeting in Nice between Charles and François, with Paul officiating. The kiss of peace was exchanged and Charles was allowed to return home by traversing France. François hoped that in exchange for his permission Charles would, in a gesture of brotherly affection, accord him Milan. Charles felt that entrusting himself to François was proof enough of their shared love.

Pope Paul had another brilliant idea. He got his son, Pier Luigi Farnese, to offer Charles 2,000,000 ducats for Milan that Pier Luigi wanted for *his* son, Ottavio Farnese, who was already Charles' son-in-law, having married Charles' daughter Margaret, Alessandro de' Medici's widow. We learn much more about Pier Luigi Farnese elsewhere, but for the moment I would like to take an instructive detour in order to explain exactly who Alessandro de' Medici was and how he met his death, a detour taken from my book *Cellini*:

Alessandro, age 19, was named to rule Florence by his father Pope Clement VII. Alessandro took advice from no one, living for his own pleasure, his motto being "They made me duke, so I'll enjoy it!" By enjoying it he meant wandering the streets at night fully armed, pushing aside anyone in his way, looking for a fight he was destined to win for the simple reason that he had barred the carrying of a sword or a firearm, both of which never left him, nor did his dagger. And he had reason to fear, as the nobility of Florence wanted him replaced by legitimate blood, noble blood. He had gained power and had by now fully tasted every perversion, so that what was left was taking the hymen of those who still had one, notably nuns, and that of those who kept guard over theirs, virtuous women. He liked his boys too, for quick, easy couplings, as heated and virile as possible. His favorite companion was his cousin Lorenzino with whom he shared his bed and more after a night of joint whoring. And when he awoke with a lustful urge, Lorenzino was always conveniently spread out, naked, at his side. This is how Cellini had caught them many times, as the artist was permitted to come and go as he wished, and as Alessandro had no modesty and no need to hide his vices, Cellini was aware of everything that took place. ''Meanwhile I went on making the Duke's portrait and oftentimes I found him napping after dinner with that Lorenzino of his.''

Lorenzino, at times, behind his back, was called Lorenzaccio, ''bad Lorenzo,'' for his habit of cutting off the heads of statues and other misdemeanors, clear proof that he shared much of Alessandro's waywardness, at least at the beginning.

No one knows why Lorenzino turned against Duke Alessandro, aided by a professional assassin, Scoronconcolo. In his play Musset writes that he wanted the duke dead so that Florence could again become a Republic. Others suggest that he was just jealous of the duke's powers and privileges. As Duke Alessandro was so unpopular, he was never without his body armor, weapons and guards. But Lorenzino told him that he had found a Florentine lady of exception beauty and, especially, ironclad virtue. Lorenzino would bring her to the duke, and from then on it was up to the duke to prove that he could triumph over purity. Lorenzino convinced the duke to dismiss the guards for the night, to take off his armor and to slip naked into bed. From then on it was easy for Lorenzino to strike him with a dagger. Afterwards he rode off to Venice, a glove covering a finger Alessandro had nearly bitten off. There, he published his version of what had taken place in his *Apologia*, claiming to be a second Brutus. Lorenzino himself was later stabbed to death by a poisoned dagger on a bridge in Venice.

Now that Alessandro is rightly dead, as they put it at the time, let's get back to our story of the Renaissance Wars.

Charles was tempted to accept the 2,000,000 ducats for Milan, and in truth he should have as it was the destiny of Milan to be an eternal headache. While this was going on François was busy trying to conquer Nice using French and Ottoman troops, to the disbelief of Christian Europe. François had even turned over the French natural port of Toulon to Barbarossa, a bloodthirsty murderer of Christian children and women, only second to the Great Khan. Charles sent Spanish ships to reinforce Nice, thusly thwarting François' plans. To avenge himself, François decided to return to reclaim Milan. Thrilled at the call of battle, infinitely more exciting than the call of the hunt, French boys, mostly still adolescents, begged their king for permission to join his ranks, and François naturally agreed. French met Spanish on Italian soil at Ceresole, the French seconded by Swiss mercenaries, the Spanish by Germans. There was even a crop of new Florentine lads, Juan-Borgia clones (3), there in favor of Charles. The weapons of choice were harquebusiers and pistoliers, lances and pikes and arrows. The French and the Swiss were the most redoubtable, and soon the Spanish and the Germans were throwing down their arms and seeking shelter among the horses of the French cavalry, deemed more humane than the Swiss and French troops who were mercilessly ending the lives of all who crossed their path. 15,000 of Charles' men were said to have died, a drop in the bucket in what the Spanish and the Florentines and the Germans and the Swiss had still to offer in the endless generations nurtured on soil drenched in blood.

While awaiting this new generation of cannon fodder, Charles and François signed the Peace of Crépy where all territories taken since their meeting at Nice would be returned. Thousands of sacrificed lives for absolutely nothing. Charles needed money and needed to take care of unrest in Germany; François needed to deal with Henry VIII who had taken Boulogne. A marriage between Charles and François' offspring was set for some unspecified future.

The year was 1547. 12 years remained of the Renaissance Wars.

Then François died, and Henry VIII too. François' son Henry II was a good boy and king, but no François I. Edward VI of England was a good boy too, but dead at age 16, replaced by his sister Mary who would wed Charles V's son Philip. Not until Elizabeth would England be a problem again to the Spanish, or to anyone else.

What took place next were tiny disputes in localities with names such as Brà, Bene, Asti and others. Charles took Siena and lost it and took it back. The Sienese were reduced to such misery that Charles ruled over a city of skeletons, a city known then, as it is today, as one of the most civilized and cultured in Italy. Charles resigned power over to Philip who was good at what he did but no Charles. The French did take Corsica, for a while, before taking it permanently in 1769, making Napoleon French, to the apparent joy of French mothers who could witness their sons, thousands upon thousands of them, sacrifice their brief lives *pour la gloire de la patrie.*

Charles V, Henry VIII, François I and Julius II left the stage, and the stage went silent.

Peace came with the treaty of Cateau-Cambrésis. The year was 1559. The Renaissance Wars were over.

The Calling of Matthew

The painting is wonderful: the ochres, the beauty of Christ and the men, but equally wonderful is its interpretation. Christ is pointing a finger at Matthew and is saying ''Follow me,'' and with biblical simplicity it is written, ''And Matthew rose and followed Him.'' But which of the men is in reality Matthew, is unknown. Christ seems to be pointing at a bearded man who was also the model for Matthew in *The Martyrdom of Saint Matthew* and *The Inspiration of Saint Matthew*. Yet Christ could just as well be pointing to a young man whose head is slumped over the table, a moment before he raises it and sees Christ. Interestingly, Christ's gesture, when pointing at Matthew, is an exact replica of God pointing to Adam in Michelangelo's *The Creation of Adam* in the Sistine Chapel.

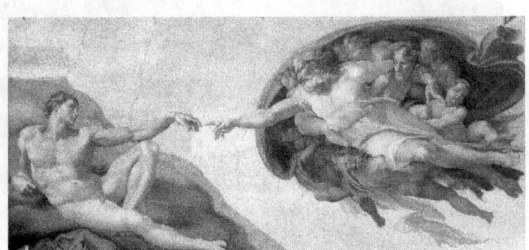

Michelangelo's *The Creation of Adam.*

The commission for the painting was at first offered to Caravaggio's old mentor, Cavalier d'Arpino, by the church of San Luigi dei Francesi in Rome, but as he was too busy, Caravaggio received the command. The painting was paid for by Cardinal Matteo Contarelli (a Frenchman whose real name was Mathieu Cointrel) who had supposedly saved for years to have a picture of his namesake: Matteo/Mathieu/Matthew. Del Monte had pulled the necessary strings to get Caravaggio the job, the result of which would make Caravaggio's name known to those who counted, launching him to fame and fortune.

As usual with Caravaggio, the detail is stupefying, right down to the dirt-embedded bare feet and grime in the toenails. The realism is again proof that mannerism and the baroque stuck to Caravaggio like water on a duck's back. The boy leaning on the old man's shoulder, by the way, is Caravaggio's lover Mario Minniti.

Caravaggio situated his personages on the primed canvas without preparatory drawings. Da Vinci and Michelangelo left behind hundreds of drawings. Caravaggio none.

The interior of the church San Luigi dei Francesi is dark, and Caravaggio made the painting dark in an attempt to bring out the central figures illuminated in such a way that one's eyes are immediately drawn to them. The painting is truly an ideal study of Caravaggio's use of chiaroscuro.

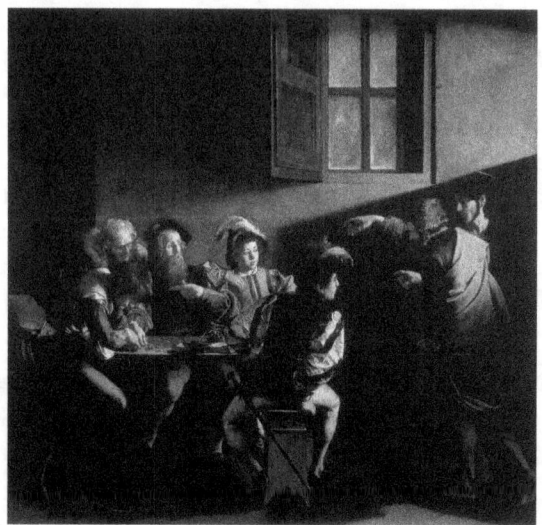

The Calling of Matthew

CHAPTER SEVEN

CURTAIN

- 1 -

Caravaggio spent a year on Sicily. He came upon his old bar-hopping, whore-frequenting, street-brawling pal and lover, Mario Minniti, who had calmed himself enough to establish his own well-considered workshop, earning the patronage of the island's Who's Who, which had transformed Minniti into a gentleman. Caravaggio went from one city to another, some say in near panic, but the exact nature of the threat is unknown. The Knights were all over the island, their ships in every major harbor. Had Wignacourt wished him ill, Caravaggio would have been easily recaptured or killed. But to make certain the Fates were on his side, Caravaggio nonetheless sent Wignacourt a peace offering in the form of a painting. We don't know who was tracking him down. We'll never know.

From Syracuse he went (fled according to one source) to Messina. As the island was too dangerous to be covered on foot, he sailed. Even common farmers, historians claim, would robe, ransom or murder a traveler without hesitation or scruple. Sicilians were vindictive and quarrelsome; the women built like summa wrestlers, the men as skinny as twigs, claimed one writer. Caravaggio is thought to have sailed in winter, the time that boats were most likely to be shipwrecked, proof of what he considered an urgency.

Messina was fortified to such an extent that the inhabitants were said to have scoffed at the threat of a Turkish invasion. It was described as wondrously beautiful ... until a succession of earthquakes leveled it.

As usual (and especially in times of troubles), Caravaggio worked. He was known on the island as he was everywhere else, and commissions piled up. From 200 scudi per painting he had gone to 400, a thousand, and now 2,000 was considered a bargain. Caravaggio spent a good part of it on earthy delights, we learn, perhaps making up for Malta where the young aristocrats were too proud and arrogant to give themselves sexually to a mere painter, and where, anyway, such relations were severely punished. He supposedly made up for lost time now in Messina. Besides visiting the taverns and back streets known for their vice, he was denounced for his too assiduous interest in the lads bathing nude in the port, and indeed had hired several to pose and otherwise entertain him. He was forced to leave quickly when right-thinking citizens rose up in force against him. Graham-Dixon calls the episode concerning his voyeurism *weird*. I'm not sure what he means, but one of the simplest pleasures in life is, and has always been, the sight of naked lads frolicking in rivers and lakes. For boys' insouciant laughter is like the ringing of church bells, and their carefree fun--they who must labor daily and often die for their country--is an untold joy. For someone who appreciates the beauty of boys, the spectacle is beyond words.

He went to Palermo where he embarked for Naples by way of glorious Capri and Ischia. Back on familiar ground, he didn't lose time in returning to the Osteria del Ciriglio, a tavern in a back alley of Naples frequented by both the dregs of society and the upper-class slumming for sex, a place known for its orgies, possessing a secret door for men who preferred boys, a door Caravaggio took as he certainly took the lad or lads within. But after one of these visits, on his way out, he was waylaid by a group of men who beat him up and then badly scarred his face, a fate reserved for whores. No one knows who these men were. Had they been sent by Roero he would have been murdered. Had Wignacourt been responsible he would have been punished in exactly this way as Wignacourt would have wanted revenge, not his death. Some put blame on the family and friends of Ranuccio Tomassoni, but the Tomassoni family was stationed in Rome and logistically it would have been difficult for them to organize an attack in Naples.

It was perhaps in Naples that Caravaggio did his darkest painting, *David with the Head of Goliath*.

- 2 -

Caravaggio was naturally influenced by his times, but I believe he was especially a law unto himself. Raised alone, free from parental authority, he quite simply forged his own character.

Cellini was a son so desired by his father that he was christened *Benvenuto*, and from then on a father's love metamorphosed into worship. Caravaggio had no such luck, and the love he could give others suffered from the inadequacy.

Caravaggio was, indisputably, a genius, far more so in painting than Michelangelo (although in sculpture Michelangelo and Bernini are untouchable gods, as is Cellini in bronze), certainly less intellectual than da Vinci, as sensual in his love of boys as Cellini although, perhaps, less loving. Michelangelo said himself that he worked more than any man who had ever lived, and I believe this to be true. But Caravaggio was second on the list. His *oeuvre*, for such a short life, is incomparable.

The *chiaro* beauty of earthly things that surrounded Caravaggio, the beauty of the Italy he knew and the Italian boys he loved and who graced his life--a gold and azure setting to his chiaroscuro painting--is the incontestable proof of the reality of God; the *obscuro* obscurity of his mind and the hatred in his heart is the equally incontestable proof that no god worthy of the name could possible exist.

Of the lesser players, Caravaggio's sidekick in fighting and whoring, Onorio Longhi, died of syphilis. His exceedingly beautiful model and whore friend Fillide died wealthy, perhaps too of syphilis. Prospero Orsi continued his life as a painter whose works also include the Vatican Library. He died at age 75. Orazio Gentileschi painted in Rome before going to Genoa, Paris and ending his life in the court of Charles I of England, he and his three sons members of the Buckingham household (13). After Buckingham's assassination his commands came directly from Charles' wife Henrietta. Constanza Colonna was faithful to Caravaggio to the end, for which she's earned a place in my heart until my own end which I hope--like that requested by Caesar the night before his assassination, while dining with Brutus--will be rapid and unexpected.

Mario Minniti retired to his native Sicily where, as said earlier, he opened a workshop that literally flooded the island with works of art, making Minniti Sicily's most important artist. He welcomed Caravaggio to his home near the end of Caravaggio's life, when Caravaggio was fleeing both a murder conviction and someone from Malta set on killing him.

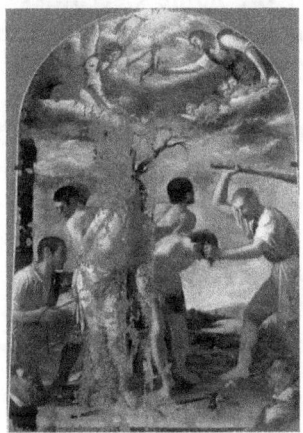

The Martyrdom of Four Saints by Mario Minniti.

Minniti was a sidekick of Caravaggio, one who roamed the streets looking for trouble, as well as the main figure in *The Musicians,* in the throes of orgasm, his eyes glazed over, his mouth ecstatically ajar while emitting a sigh, his tongue sensually visible, his cheeks lustfully reddened. He and Caravaggio had been young together, in Rome, both experiencing the ups-and-downs inherent in life but, being young, they were armed against all eventualities, armed by their youth.

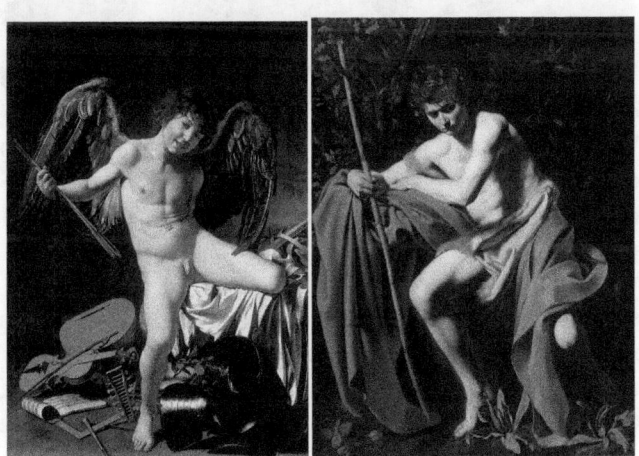

Cecco in *Love Conquers All* and *John the Baptist.*

Cecco was not only Caravaggio's belovèd, he learned from the master and then went on to create important works of his own. There are doubts that he was treated as lovingly by Caravaggio as were the boys of da Vinci and Cellini--or Michelangelo when Michelangelo was in love--but we'll never know. His real name seems to have been Francesco Boneri ou Buoneri, but he adopted the name Cecco del Caravaggio. He's thought to have been French by some, Spanish by others, Italian by most. He was John in *St. John the Baptist* and the joyful boy in *Love Conquers All*. Some authorities think he was the boy holding Goliath's head in *David with the Head of Goliath*, others believe the boy was a self-portrait of Caravaggio, as he remembered himself. The difference between the brooding lad in *St. John the Baptist* and the carefree boy in *Love Conquers All* is truly heart wrenching. In *Love* he is too young to feel the weight of the world as he does in *John*.

Cecco vanished from history, having lived a life of infinite rebounds, sharing the air and more with a wondrous, enigmatic artist, known as Caravaggio.

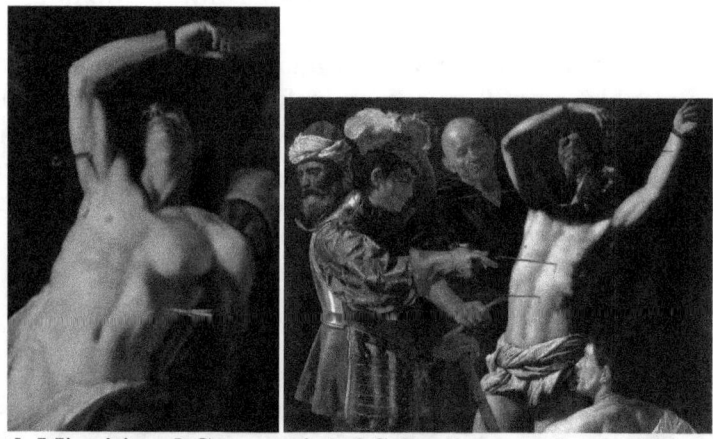

Both Minniti and Cecco painted Sebastians, and coincidentally Caravaggio's remains were laid to rest in a chapel near where he died, a chapel dedicated to the poor. Its name? St. Sebastian.

Besides being disfigured during the attack in front of the Osteria del Ciriglio, Caravaggio was perhaps even partially blinded. His convalescence at the Colonna Palace near Naples took six months. It was then that he painted what was one of the darkest paintings of a lifetime of dark masterpieces, his *Martyrdom of St. Ursula,* that I described at the beginning of this book.

Word came from Rome for him to return. Glory would once more be his. Scipione had commissions by the bucketful. He would be pardoned. He would be acknowledged and rewarded as the greatest living painter. He would be enriched as only Michelangelo had before him. His knighthood would be reestablished. The young twerps on Malta would be obliged to kowtow despite their nobility--the gift of accidental birth, not merit. And, of course, there would be boys without end, the husky lads of the countryside, the lithe boys of the towns, the red-blooded glory of glorious Italy.

He sailed from Naples to Rome. Why he landed farther north of Rome, at perhaps Palo, is unknown. An ill wind in the form of a gale perhaps blew him off course. He landed and was arrested for being a bandit, perhaps due to his clothes, always thread bare, and the cuts that disfigured his face, following the attack at the Osteria del Ciriglio. When he was released he learned his boat had gone to Porto Ercole. He went after it, perhaps on foot, perhaps he had enough money on him after his arrest to hire a mule, although the arresting guards had most probably appropriated his valuables. Some sources believe he made it that far. Others that, ill and in deep sufferance from his Ciriglio wounds, he was taken in at a hut along the way. This man, so clearly cut out for a violent death by sword or dagger died, at age 38, of fever, as Virgil had off the coast of Brindisi. The light went out for them both, an eternal loss to the world. Caravaggio was a man who certainly abused life, but one that allowed life, in its turn, to use him-- for me the paramount accolade.

Final Interlude

David with the Head of Goliath

Painted in the year of his death, 1610, *David with the Head of Goliath* is Caravaggio's most stunning painting: David a small lithe boy, deadly solemn, showing neither fear nor awe at having decapitated the giant, certainly no regret killing the Philistine heathen, thanks to which David would become king of Israel. The painting is moving in many senses. Did Caravaggio have a premonition of his coming end, and wish to join both extremities of his time on earth, he as a boy in the form of David, he as an older man, dead in one dull, sightless eye, a glint of still-existent life in the other, his mouth ajar in an eternally silenced scream, his face still lacerated from the beating in front of the Osteria del Ciriglio? Or was David his lover Cecco, his shirt open and in disarray as in life, a child he had ''known'' at age 10, had painted again and again as he grew into manhood, finally portrayed here from memory, the inextinguishable memory of a lover, Caravaggio, for his belovèd, Cecco? Caravaggio had called David *il suo caravaggino*, his little Caravaggio, which could have meant Cecco, who later adopted Caravaggio's name, or it could have meant Caravaggio as he was as a little boy.

Caravaggio offered the painting to Scipione Borghese, a friend, a patron, and the official power who held Caravaggio's blood-dripping head in his hands, as did David, in that Scipione had the power to have

Caravaggio cleared of killing Tommasoni … or have him decapitated. Scipione was known as an ardent lover of boys. Some suggest that he would have recognized David's uplifted sword as an erect member, a reminder of what the cardinal and the artist held in common, a detail Caravaggio had added, on purpose to please Scipione. On the sword is written H-As OS, *Humilitas occidit superbiam*, humility shall kill pride. The painting remains in the Borghese Palace to this day.

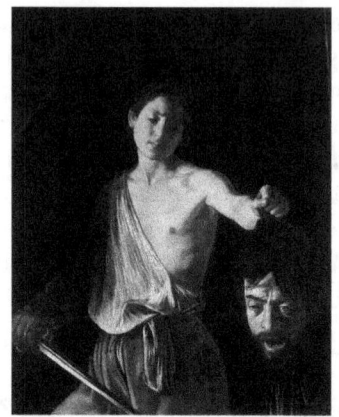

David with the Head of Goliath

SOURCES

(1) See my book *Renaissance Homosexuality.*
(2) See my book *Alcibiades.*
(3) See my book *Cesare Borgia.*
(4) See my book *TROY.*
(5) See my autobiography *Michael Hone, His World, His Loves.*
(6) See my book *Cellini.*
(7) See my book *Greek Homosexuality.*
(8) See my book *Roman Homosexuality.*
(9) See my book *The History of Orgies.*
(10) See my book *Henry III.*
(11) See my book *Christ Had His John, I Have My George.*
(12) See my book *Sebastian.*
(13) See my book *Buckingham.*

Ady Cecilia, *A History of Milan under the Sforza,* 1907.
Aldrich Robert and Garry Wotherspoon, *Who's Who in Gay and Lesbian*

History, 2001.

Baglione, *Caravaggio*, circa 1600.

Bellori, *Caravaggio*, circa 1600.

Bergreen Laurence, *Over the Edge of the World – Magellan's Terrifying Circumnavigation of the Globe*, 2003.

Bicheno Hugh, *Vendetta, High Art and Low Cunning at the Birth of the Renaissance*, 2007.

Bramly Serge, *Leonardo*, 1988. I hesitated to order the book due to its date of publication, but that would have been a great mistake as it's not only beautifully written, it's marvelously complete. Bramly, no prude, covers in depth da Vinci's homosexuality. An absolute must.

Cawthorne, Nigel, *Sex Lives of the Popes*, 1996.

Chamberlin, E.R. *The Fall of the House of Borgia*, 1974.

Cloulas Ivan, *The Borgia*, 1989.

Crowley Roger, *Empires of the Sea*, 2008. Marvelous.

Forellino Antonio, *Michelangelo*, 2005. The most beautiful reproductions I've ever seen in a book, but nearly nothing about Michelangelo's homosexuality.

Jack Belinda, *Beatrice's Spell*, 2004.

Johnson, Marion, *The Borgias*, 1981.

Gayford Martin, *Michelangelo*, 2013. A beautiful book, wonderfully written. Michelangelo's homosexuality so evenhandedly covered that I had to look up Gayford to see if he was gay--with a wife and children he apparently isn't. A must, must read.

Graham-Dixon Andrew, *Caravaggio, A Life Sacred and Profane*, 2010. The book is fabulous. A genuine I-couldn't-put-it-down.

Grazia Sebastian de, *Machiavelli in Hell*, 1989.

Guicciardini, *Storie fiorentine (History of Florence)*, 1509. An absolute must-read.

Hibbert Christopher, *The Borgias and Their Enemies*, 2009. I love everything he writes.

Hibbert Christopher, *The Rise and Fall of the House of Medici*, 1974.

Hibbert Christopher, *Florence, the Biography of a City*, 1993.

Lambert Gilles *Caravaggio*, 2007.

Landucci Luca, *A Florentine Diary*, around 1500, an apothecary who wrote about Florence and is today a vital source concerning his times.

Lev Elizabeth, *The Tigress of Forli*, 2011. Wonderfully written. I love Elizabeth Lev for having giving us this marvelous work about this incredible woman.

Levy Buddy, *River of Darkness*, 2011. Fabulous.

Lubkin Gregory, *A Renaissance Court*, 1994.

Mallett Michael and Christine Shaw, *The Italian Wars 1494-1559*.

Manchester William, *A World Lit Only By Fire*, 1993.

Mancini, *Caravaggio*, circa 1600.

Martines Lauro, *April Blood-Florence and the Plot against the Medici*, 2003. A magnificent book, I've reread it three times.

Meyer G.J. *The Borgias, The Hidden History*, 2013.

Noel Gerard, *The Renaissance Popes*, 2006.

Parker Derek, *Cellini*, 2003, the book is beautifully written and full of reproductions. The very, very best on this fabulous artist.

Robb Peter, *Street Fight in Naples*, 2010.

Robb Peter, M – *The Man Who Became Caravaggio*, 1998.

Rocke Michael, *Forbidden Friendships*, 1996, both indispensible and wonderful. Rocke has become *incontournable*.

Sabatini Rafael, *The Life of Cesare Borgia*, 1920.

Saslow James, *Ganymede in the Renaissance*, 1986.

Seward Desmond, *Caravaggio – A Passionate Life*, 1998.

Simonetta Marcello, *The Montefeltro Conspiracy*, 2008. Wonderful, wonderful, wonderful.

Strathern Paul, *The Medici, Godfathers of the Renaissance*, 2003, An absolute must-read.

Unger Miles, *Machiavelli*, 2008.

Unger Miles, *Magnifico, The Brilliant Life and Violent Times Of Lorenzo de' Medici*, 2011. Wonderful. The best.

Vasari: We would know next to nothing if it were not for this great man (even if he does scratch his boys during sex [6]).

Viroli Maurizio, *Niccolo's Smile, A Biography of Machiavelli*, 1998.

Weir Alison, *The Princes in the Tower*, 1992. Marvelous.

Wikipedia: Research today is impossible without the aid of this monument.

Wright Ed, *History's Greatest Scandals*, 2006.

Wroe Ann, *Perking, A Story of Deception*, 2003. Fabulous

INDEX

Please note that the page numbers are *passim*. An example, Cecco 76 – 102 means that Cecco is found within these pages, but not necessarily on *every* page.